Spying on Success

Competitive Intelligence

in the

Age of Artificial Intelligence

SECOND EDITION

Michael Schrenk

Published by

Mepso Media LLC, Nevada USA

www.mepso.com

Second Edition, October 2025
First Edition, April 2024

Spying on Success

Competitive Intelligence in the age of Artificial Intelligence
Second Edition

Hardcover	ISBN: 979-8-9934831-0-8
Paperback	ISBN: 979-8-9934831-2-2
Kindle	ASIN: B0FSFL2SXX

| Author | Michael Schrenk |
| Production Assistant | Cali Chihaupom |

© 2025 Mepso Media LLC

Please contact the publisher for:

- Permission and Review copies
- Speaker inquiries and Interview requests
- Group sales and language translations

The content of this book is provided for informational purposes only. While Mepso Media makes every effort to ensure the accuracy and timeliness of the information presented, neither the publisher nor the author makes any guarantees regarding its completeness, accuracy, reliability, suitability, or availability. All information, products, services, and related materials are provided "as is."

Mepso Media LLC
Las Vegas, Nevada USA
www.mepso.com

Contact the author at: mike@mepso.com

i 1 2 3 4 5 6 7 8 9 0 A B C   2 0 0 0 1 0

Thank you Gramma.

Charlotte Schrenk
1897-1982

Introduction

While his competitors were busy fulfilling online sales, *Mitch Modell* (the CEO of *Modell's Sporting Goods),* was still trying to navigate the transition from brick-and-mortar retail to eCommerce. His three-generation business had grown to 150 stores, from New York to Virginia, but none of that prepared him for the Internet.

He heard that his main competitor had developed a process called, *"Ship From Store".*[1] This program allowed his rival to use individual stores, located across the country, as distribution points for website sales.

Shipping orders from existing stores sounded like an obvious competitive advantage. But, stores aren't arranged like distribution centers. Additionally, brick-and-mortar retail doesn't have a process that resembles order fulfillment. The solution to using stores as online distribution centers wasn't as obvious as it sounded. Mr. Modell knew the answer was out there. He just had to do some research.

So one crisp February morning, Mitch shed his identity as the head of his family-owned sporting goods business and pretended to be an executive from his larger competitor, *Dick's Sporting Goods.*[1] He arrived at his competitor's store in full disguise, complete with a fake mustache and a junior assistant. On his arrival, he introduced himself as a traveling Vice President and claimed he had a meeting later that morning with

---

[1] Dick's: Modell's CEO posed as exec to get secrets | 6abc Philadelphia | 6abc.com. (2021, September 30). 6abc Philadelphia. https://6abc.com/archive/9448941/

their CEO.[2]

Eager to please a visiting executive, a group of employees led Mr. Modell and his assistant to an office containing files he had asked to study before his supposed meeting. The staff offered assistance and answered any questions he had.

While this caper took some planning, the endgame was clearly less defined. Eventually, the employees discovered that the man they were assisting wasn't who he said he was. The police were called and shortly after Mr. Modell and his assistant were both charged with several counts of civil conspiracy. Perhaps worse than that, his community-focused business had to deal with the reaction to a very public mistake.

The case was settled out-of-court. And it was settled very quickly, indicating that Modell had to accept a pretty bleak set of conditions, which likely helped lead to the eventual downfall of the business.

What makes a strange story even stranger is that Mr. Modell also performed a similar stunt on US national television, where he appeared on the CBS show *Undercover Boss*. Here again, he wore a fake mustache, shaved his head, and pretended to be an entry-level employee. But this time to spy on his employees.[3]

Or, maybe the story wasn't as strange as it sounds. Perhaps he felt that the potential competitive intelligence was so valuable that the risk was acceptable?

---

[2] ABC News. (2014, March 5). Dick's Sporting Goods accuses rival modell's of spying. *ABC News*. https://abcnews.go.com/Business/dicks-sporting-goods-accuses-rival-modells-spying/story?id=22756803

[3] As an aside, the story is also deeply ironic. The one thing that could have saved this business was the COVID epidemic, when people bought home fitness gear at unprecedented levels. Ironically, COVID's only effect on Modell's was that it postponed their liquidation sale. And in another ironic note, the brand was purchased during the liquidation and now the only part of the company that remains is the website (minus the retail stores).

As you'll see. There are better ways to conduct competitive intelligence campaigns.

Contents

C hapter 1
What is competitive intelligence?

Competitive intelligence creates advantages from information that other businesses ignore, or don't have the wherewithal to process. Competitive intelligence works by capitalizing on both unintentional communication and market dynamics.

Use QR code to access video, "What is Competitive Intelligence?"

The awareness gained through competitive intelligence equips organizations with the resources needed to make better decisions in three main areas.

In markets where you sell, competitive intelligence will help you better understand your customers. You'll be better equipped to locate markets and justify pricing.

In markets where you buy, competitive intelligence can locate prime inventory, and buy it before anyone else finds it. Or, CI can provide advance warnings of supply line issues.

Competitive intelligence can also provide advance knowledge of threats, or find new places to compete.

In short, competitive intelligence helps organizations better understand the environments where they compete, by transforming vague data into actionable intelligence that creates competitive advantages.

Competitive intelligence's value

In 2024 Intel disclosed annual losses of $7 billion due to poor strategic planning.[4] The cited article specifically claims that Intel admitted that a "lack of competitive knowledge" attributed to years of bad decision making.

Competitive intelligence is important enough that 64% of organizations spend at least $25,000 on it every year[5]. Outside of direct expenditures, competitive intelligence is often baked into Marketing, or Search Engine Optimization, where knowledge of one's physical and virtual markets are required.

Competitive intelligence doesn't just find better ways to compete, it also can gauge how well you're performing in your market by determining your market share. Knowing who controls your markets is fundamental to knowing how well you're managing your business. Market share reports provide many opportunities to compare and contrast how businesses are managed.

The attraction to competitive intelligence

Modell's Sporting Goods was desperate for intelligence on the Ship From Store program. Otherwise, why would a high-profile individual (with a good job) risk a felony prosecution and jeopardize a three-generation business to acquire competitive intelligence, especially when better tactics existed.

---

[4] Intel discloses $7 billion operating loss for chip-making unit | Reuters. (n.d.). https://www.reuters.com/technology/intel-discloses-financials-foundry-business-2024-04-02/

[3] Nichols, M. (2022, February 22). CI teams & budgets are growing faster than ever. *Crayon*. https://www.crayon.co/blog/competitive-intelligence-teams-budgets-growing-quickly

The desire to discover a competitor's trade secrets, or competitive advantages, is completely warranted and ethical as long as that discovery is done through simple observation and study. But one has to wonder what *Cost Benefit Analysis* occurred before they decided to infiltrate a competitor's ranks.

Other than: the disguise, the deceit, and an embarrassing appearance on a national TV show, perhaps the most unbelievable aspect of Modell's clandestine activity is that it occurred just a few years ago. By the year of the incursion, nearly all competitive intelligence campaigns had moved online; largely because that's where the data moved. Modell's could have gathered the same, or even better intelligence about the "Ship From Store" program by making online observations and doing some simple analysis.

Distinctions from business intelligence

Competitive intelligence stems from businesses intelligence but has since morphed into its own discipline. The main difference between business intelligence and competitive intelligence is that business intelligence is internal facing while competitive intelligence is focused on what's happening outside of your organization.

Here are a few examples of ways problems are approached differently by business and competitive intelligence.

	Business Intelligence	Competitive Intelligence
New Product Launch	Calculates production costs	Determines a competitive price
Business Expansion	Estimates how many employees your expansion plans require	Approximates labor cost, where found, and retention rates

Distinctions between BI and CI

Business intelligence can help fine tune internal processes to make your business operate efficiently. Conversely, competitive intelligence is concerned with what happens outside your organizational walls. Competitive intelligence can ensure:

- That your products are competitively priced,
- That you're offering the competitive products and services.
- You know where employees can be found and what they will cost.
- That you know in advance about the emergence of:
  - New competitors,
  - Competing product releases, or
  - Your chief competitor's expansion (or contraction) plans.

Metadata

A word you'll be reading a lot is *metadata*. While the subject of metadata is vast, for now it's enough to know that metadata has several properties.

- Metadata describes, or provides context for, other data.
- Metadata can be purely parametric, like the XIF data that is used to describe digital photographs,
- Metadata can be created through analytics.
- Metadata even exists in the absence of other data.

Later you'll learn how metadata is created and why metadata is often more useful than the source data it describes.

The nature of spying

Not all spying activities are the same. There a difference between better understanding ones markets and generally snooping around.

The difference between legitimate intelligence collection and snooping often comes down to objectives. For example, imagine a jealous spouse who timestamps and logs every interaction their spouse has on social media. This person's intent is clear, but their objective is pretty murky as it exhibits a betrayal of confidence.

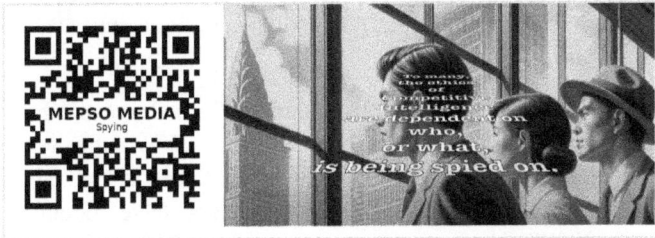

Use QR code to access video, "The Nature of Spying"

Now contrast that scenario to one where you are an executive with unverified reports that a new, and well funded, competitor has decided to move into your territory and compete for your business. But you don't know when or how much they're investing in your market. Additionally, you've delayed your own expansion plans because you're not sure how heavy the new competition will be. So you commission a competitive intelligence campaign to monitor your competitor's online job postings for new positions they'll need in your territory.

This data is analyzed to obtain intelligence that predicts when they plan to start operations, what skills they're hiring, and to what scale they are building out their business in your market. An unplanned benefit of the campaign is that your Human Resources department obtain insights into how a competitor staffs a new project. From the viewpoint of the corporate executive, the competitive intelligence campaign was done to protecting the organization's investment. Keeping an eye on your competitors is not snooping, it's a responsibility. And in these situations, it's important for organizations to have trusted sources of intelligence.

Intelligence ethics

To many, the ethics of competitive intelligence are dependent on who or what is being spied on. Some people, myself included, believe that there is a responsibility to monitor powerful entities that have influence over economies and politics. In contrast, spying on individuals is an invasion of individual privacy.

While there is a healthy discussion of the balance between investigation and privacy, less is said about the legal obligations officers of corporations have to their shareholders and employees. Since corporate officers have fiduciary responsibilities to investors, they are expected to use the best and most current information available to make strategic decisions. Decision makers have an actual legal reason to spy on their competitors, because competitive intelligence is required to make informed decisions.

Spycraft

The mysteries surrounding intelligence sometimes promote the myth that competitive intelligence uses exciting spycraft. You might be surprised to find that intelligence gathering is hard to differentiate from regular office work. This is especially true if your intelligence is Internet based, as it's apt to be. Yet, competitive intelligence is often conflated with espionage.

It's easy to see how the connection between competitive intelligence and espionage happens because they *feel similar* and they do have some commonalities.

But unlike competitive intelligence, espionage is conducted covertly and often involves intelligence agencies or bots that operate secretly to detect and collect sensitive information. But that's where the similarities end. Competitive intelligence and espionage have different objectives and capabilities.

Espionage, by definition, must involve intelligence collection between nation states. So unless your competitor is a governmental entity, competitive intelligence is not technically espionage.

The competitive intelligence conundrum

The only time the public hears about competitive intelligence is when unethical campaigns, like the one in the introduction, are discovered and reported in the news. This gives competitive intelligence an undeserved public relations problem. You'll hear about the failures, because they can be spectacular. But you'll seldom hear of the competitive intelligence success stories because these campaigns are tightly guarded *trade secrets* that don't have conventional intellectual property protections. (You actively need to protect trade secrets.)

The reality is that people conduct competitive intelligence naturally and without thinking about it. It's baked into our DNA to observe and take action based on observations.

Every time a poker player calculates the odds of a winning hand, that player is using competitive intelligence.

Anytime you drive an extra ten minutes to buy a discounted item, you exercise competitive intelligence.

You could say that competitive intelligence is as much a survival skill as it is a business practice.

C hapter 2

Modern collection techniques

Not so long ago, conducting a competitive intelligence campaign meant a trip to the patent library. Or maybe one would try to sniff-out a poorly guarded trade secret from a competitor's booth at a trade show. In those days, investigators needed to be physically present to conduct a competitive intelligence campaign. But that has changed.

The competitive intelligence revolution

Today, very little competitive intelligence collection is done by investigators on the street. Nearly all CI has moved online. And the move from the physical world to the virtual world is the biggest thing to happen to competitive intelligence.

The advantages to online intelligence gathering include:

- Anonymity
- Remote access
- Automation

The ability to conduct competitive intelligence anonymously, remotely, and with automation tools is relatively new. And any of these may have saved the failed campaign described in the introduction.

The rise of OSINT

Before things start sounding overly covert, this is a good time to remind ourselves that nearly all information used in online competitive intelligence is gathered from public, or Open

Source places. In other words, competitive intelligence often uses data left in public view, with no illusion or expectation of privacy. While Open Source data is available to anyone, it's only competitive intelligence consultants that find competitive advantages in publicly available data. There's more to know about *OSINT*, or *Open Source Intelligence in* Chapter 10.

Anonymity

Online intelligence collection is mostly anonymous. When done correctly, there is little likelihood of becoming discovered. Discovery is a bad for three reasons.

1. It's embarrassing

2. Once your competitor discovers your collection strategy, they are apt to develop countermeasures to foil your tradecraft.

3. When your competitor discovers your campaign, you reveal a trade secret that you never intended to lose.

Anonymity isn't gained by being sneaky. It's achieved by nicely mixing in with normal network traffic. After all, it's important to be civil in public places.

Remote access

Another advantage of online intelligence collection is that it is always done remotely. So unlike the investigators in the introduction, you don't have to infiltrate a competitor to learn about their operations. You simply need to observe what they do publicly online. And since The Internet is global, you can investigate targets located anywhere in the world.

Automation

Since most modern intelligence gathering is done with software, it's simple to automate most collections. The ability to automate intelligence gathering might be the most powerful aspect of conducting competitive intelligence campaigns online.

Automated intelligence collection means:

- Your intelligence collection scales at a lower cost
- Your accuracy improves
- Data can be harvested periodically, allowing comparisons and contrasts with historic data. Historic data can be used to detect trends and predict future events.

If you don't automate your campaigns, you become dependent on expensive and error-prone labor to gather intelligence. These costs and errors can render campaigns inoperable.

For instance, you can create an inexpensive bot that watches a website to alert you when a strategic event occurs, like a price change or the availability of a new product. It would be impractical to hire an employee to perform this task due to the high cost and the monotonous nature of repeatedly checking the website. But a bot can perform this task 24/7 without missing a beat, at a lower cost and with 100% accuracy.

Automated intelligence is also immediately actionable. For example, if a bot finds a retail price significantly higher than yours, that same bot could be programmed to slightly raise your price while still remaining competitive. Or maybe a procurement bot finds acceptable inventory at unusually good terms. The same bot that detected the deal can also purchase the item, if it matches a predefined set of criteria. In these cases, automation reduces both the time it takes to make a decision and the period of time until one acts on that decision.

Perhaps more than anything, automation allows one to scale a campaign further than anything that could be accomplished with human labor alone.

Similarities to hacking

As you may have guessed, the tactics used in modern competitive intelligence (anonymity, remote access, and automation) also happen to be what define computer hacking.

Use QR code to access video, "From Physical to Virtual"

This association with hacking creates a real public relations problem for competitive intelligence. It seems like the only time the public hears about competitive intelligence is when someone acts unethically and gets caught. What isn't made public are the CI campaigns that provide competitive advantages through observation and insight alone. You'll never hear about these campaigns because they themselves become trade secrets.

Despite the close resemblance to hacking, competitive intelligence is a legitimate business practice and an important part of curriculum at major business schools. Competitive intelligence even has its own professional association.[6]

Artificial intelligence

This second edition of *Spying on Success* was largely inspired by the steady growth of artificial intelligence and the importance it has gained in my practice. While AI can be a powerful CI tool, artificial intelligence does not excel in all of

---

[6] Strategic Consortium of Intelligence Professionals (SCIP). (n.d.). https://www.scip.org/

the areas you may expect. And while it has change virtually every aspect of my professional life, artificial intelligence has had a lesser impact on the profession than The Internet has. But that shouldn't mean that artificial intelligence shouldn't be a highly valuable tool at your disposal. The following sections describe those areas where artificial intelligence is most useful when conducting competitive intelligence campaigns.

What is AI?

There are many claims about artificial intelligence ranging from "AI's about to exceed human intelligence", to LLMs can't be trusted because of their high *hallucination rates*. The reality is the following. The chatbots we use today, like ChatGPT, are good at many things, but they excel at pattern matching. That's why they're so good at:

- Looking things up
- Checking spelling
- Translating languages
- Composing specific types of letters
- Determining the differences between two things
- Matching the writing style of a famous writer.

While chatbots have improved their ability to get information, you never really know how fresh or accurate it is. Additionally, you don't want some assurance that an AI-powered chatbot to connect to the source anymore than another tool. For these reasons, I don't recommend using AI to gather specific facts.

Chatbots are perhaps best for grand, sweeping inquires, like any of the following.

- Summarize how major commercial paint competitors have shifted pricing, dealer incentives, and color-system marketing during the past five years. Identify which tactics most threaten our mid-market share and where margin defense is possible.

- Profile new or foreign entrants to the my commercial paint market since 2020. Describe their entry models, distribution partners, and customer acquisition patterns. Recommend proactive countermeasures or partnership opportunities to neutralize early momentum within 18 months.

- Identify open segments that competitors have yet to exploit.

- Investigate the upstream networks of the paint industry. Determine where competitors have exclusive sourcing or logistics advantages. Highlight exposure to commodity volatility or import restrictions.

- Compare how national and regional paint brands structure dealer programs: discount tiers, rebates, training, and digital ordering. Identify which competitor has the fastest channel-to-market cycle.

The ability to use such prompts and get legitimate answers back is quite remarkable. But these are also the lowest hanging fruit when using AI. Since many people will be using AI in such a way, any competitive advantages gains will soon become things one needs to do, just to remain competitive. But the real advantages of AI come to those who put it to specific uses, as shown next.

Artificial intelligence and analysis

Information is easy to process when it's all formatted numbers and text. But often the best data is embedded into images, spreadsheets, pdf documents, or other such nonlinear communication. Sometimes data professionals call this kind of data *blobs* because it lacks consistent format or structure. So, it's difficult to process a lot of found data with traditional tradecraft.

Artificial intelligence, however, is very good at analyzing media that isn't text. This was demonstrated to me one day while visiting the *Getty Villa* in *Los Angeles*.[7] I was in the garden next to a statue. Out of curiosity, I took a picture of the statue with my phone and uploaded the image to *ChatGPT* where I asked if it knew anything about the exhibit.

Not only was ChatGPT aware of the sculpture, it also knew the piece's entire provenance, the history behind the depiction, where it was located at the museum, and the names of the sculptures that existed in it's immediate proximity. From that point on, ChatGPT became one of my favorite analysis tools, especially for unformatted data.

Some of the most common tasks for artificial intelligence in competitive intelligence include the following:

Anytime one needs to interpret emotions or impressions. For example, AI is the tool to use if you want to gauge the optimism of a statement or a product review.

One of the biggest battles for an analyst is to understand one's own biases and how they interfere with quality analysis. Artificial intelligence can be prompted to be free of bias. Or conversely, it can be asked to inject bias, perhaps to model a real life situation.

Artificial intelligence can run simulations

As artificial intelligence gains more acceptance, organizations will learn how to use artificial intelligence to conduct simulations. My previous book, *Structured Prompts*, explores how to use artificial intelligence to conduct simulations and workflow automations.[8]

---

[7] J. Paul Getty Museum. (n.d.). *Getty Villa*. The J. Paul Getty Trust. Located in Pacific Palisades, Los Angeles, CA.

[8] Schrenk, M. (2025). Structured prompts: For generative artificial intelligence, simulations, and workflow automation. Mepso Media LLC.

Simulations can have a major impact on competitive intelligence campaigns in that you can test theories before committing resources to them.

Some of the AI simulations you may want to conduct include:

- Simulating how competitors might react to pricing changes, product launches, or regulatory shifts.

- Modeling the effect of supply chain disruptions or fresh competition using real-world intelligence as the baseline.

- With AI you can project potential ROI for entering new markets or adopting new technologies.

- Artificial intelligence also facilitates detecting competitor strategies based on observed patterns of behavior, filling in gaps where direct intelligence is incomplete.

> Unlike traditional competitive intelligence tools, if you want to learn how to apply artificial intelligence to a problem, all you have to do is ask it how it's done.

Ranking how I use AI

But without any doubt, the single biggest advantage I've experienced (to date) with artificial intelligence is how important it has become to software development. I use AI in every Selenium Python program (AKA: bot) I write.

I'm not a fan of *Vibe Coding*, or totally relying on a chatbots to develop software. But I am a huge fan of using ChatGPT as a programming aid in any of the following circumstances.

- When a section of code doesn't work, I may cut and paste it into ChatGPT and ask it to debug it.

- If I a need a written explanation of how a section of

python code works, I'll ask ChatGPT for the explanation.

- When I get an unfamiliar error code, I will ask ChatGPT for an explanation.

- I will ask ChatGPT to conduct code reviews of software I've written.

- If I come across some exotic, home-brewed, web control, I will ask ChatGPT how to access it. I've found this much more productive than recording the session the Selenium browser extension.

Unfortunately, this book does not explain how to write bots, as the focus is on competitive intelligence, not software development. But if you're interested in writing bots, or applying artificial intelligence to business problems, I suggest one of my earlier books. *Developing Bots with Selenium Python (2023, Mepso Media)* or *Structured Prompt's (2025, Mepso Media)*.

Further thoughts

When businesses moved online they took their bad habits with them. All of the security and privacy problems organizations in had the bricks-and-mortar world came with them when they moved online. The Internet has essentially created new opportunities for business to breach their own privacy.

In addition to moving their problems online, corporate webpages became the subject of the techniques and tools used by computer hackers, namely: the ability to investigate remotely, with anonymity, and with the benefit of automation.

C hapter 3
Setting objectives

Organizations use competitive intelligence to address a variety of concerns. But how does one match the needs of an organization with the capabilities of competitive intelligence?

This chapter covers three main areas.

- The importance of playbooks

- Common business objectives that can be addressed through competitive intelligence.

- Self-audits to reveal competitive intelligence opportunities.

Planning and playbooks

Are you ready to jump into your first competitive intelligence campaign? The excitement of developing and conducting competitive intelligence campaigns sometimes cause investigators to skip a step or two, or to not plan at all. Don't be one of those people.

Before you begin, please recognize that poorly planned competitive intelligence campaigns, regardless of potential can consume: money, energy, and as we saw in the preface, pride.

When organizations spend resources on competitive intelligence, they should expect a predictable outcome. As obvious as that sounds, I've seen many dollars and euros spent on frivolous vanity projects without any demonstrable return on investment.

Successful competitive intelligence campaigns do not just happen. They are planned and documented in a *playbook*. You might think of the playbook as the specification for your competitive intelligence campaign.

One of the tricks to keep investigators on track is to break your the campaign into three sections: Objective, Tactics, and Sources.

Every playbook should:

- State your objective. What is the specific task you're trying to accomplish and who will benefit from the campaign?

- Describe the tactics that will gather intelligence to accomplish your objective. Your tactics should describe, not only the intelligence collection process, but also how you plan to:
    - Work remotely
    - Maintain anonymity
    - Use automation

- Where are the sources of your intelligence? Do you have more than one? Multiple sources are always preferable because:
    - You have backups, if your primary source dries-up.
    - More sources also mean more data, and potentially, more meaningful statistics.

Playbooks are also a great place to make a simple ethics statement. Let it serve as a documented reminder of what your campaign *won't do*. As you will read later, lapses in ethics can not only sink a campaign, but leave the investigator with a lot of explaining to do when poor ethical decisions are discovered.

It's healthy to divide a playbook into sections that define your: Objectives, Tactics, and Sources separately because it causes the investigator to focus and concentrate on each of the aspects of the campaign individually. The goal is to do your homework first and to avoid getting overly excited about one aspect of a campaign at the expense of other considerations.

What the story in the introduction got wrong

The story in the introduction is an example of what happens when people to insufficient planning. Their objective however, to get fulfillment intelligence, was valid. They worked on anonymity (the disguise helped). And they knew a source of intelligence. Their problem was that their tactics were flawed beyond the ethics they violated.

Let's take a look a some simple tactics Modell's could have applied to achieve better intelligence, if they had chosen an online campaign.

Instead of planning to physically penetrate enemy lines, Mr. Modell could have taken advantage of an area of military security known as *OPSEC, or Operational Security*.

OPSEC is the process of studying what can be discovered about an organization by simply observing its operations. It is usually conducted internally, by a security team as a counterintelligence measure. But when OPSEC is redirected on competitors, intelligence can be pieced together to uncover trade secrets.

Today, like most competitive intelligence, OPSEC has also moved online. So in Modell's case, physically going to the competitor's store to grill the employees and drill through files was unnecessary. Just as much, or more intelligence, could have been gathered by studying their website remotely, anonymously, and with the benefit of automation.

Physical and virtual inventories are linked. So online stores are often windows into internal operations.

It may very well have been possible for Modell's to learn more about their competitor's online fulfillment program by simply using their website to selectively purchase select test products

37

and have them shipped to various locations. They could have examined the artifacts of the fulfillment and shipping process for clues as to how and where the orders were fulfilled.

Applying OPSEC

Some of the fulfillment strategies they could have tested include:

- Purchase one item from different parts of the country to discover their shipping origin.
    - Does it appear that they ship regionally or are they shipping from all their stores?
    - Are they using more than one carrier?
- If you buy all available units of a specific item:
    - Does that item's price increase?
    - Does it go out of stock?
    - Is it still in stock in other markets?
- What happens to returned merchandise?
    - If the item is returned anonymously with an Apple AirTag, can you tell where and how returned merchandise is handled?
- Do all items in an single order always originate from the same store?
- What happens if an order is placed near a store, but for an item you know is locally out of stock?
- Are seasonal and high-volume items handled differently?

At some point, Modell's may have wanted to extend their research into monitoring their competitor's prices automatically. They could then compare and contrast common inventory and prices to their own. There was a lot of relevant information that they could have collected remotely with anonymity and with automation without ever stepping inside a competitor's property (or needing to hire a lawyer and defend themselves in a court room).

Additionally, through OPSEC, they could have determined the relative market dominance of each of their competitors so they could determine if online sales helped their company to gain market share.

It's vital that your campaign is based on addressing a business objective. This is worth mentioning because people often bypass this step and substitute an objective with an urge to use an emerging tactic or hot new intelligence source. Starting with a stated objective, however, helps ensure that your campaign has a clear path to success by providing a theme that keeps your campaign on track.

Common competitive intelligence objectives

While many competitive intelligence campaigns involve industry-specific objectives, most campaigns fall into several generic categories.

Objective: Know your market share

Market share depicts the percentage of total business shared by competitors in a given territory over a specific period of time. This is an important metric because, more than others, market share gauges how well you compete. Market share is an indicator of your organization's health.

In many ways, knowing your market share is more useful than knowing if you're making money. For example, your business might make payroll every week and even generate a small profit. But it you're losing market share, it's only a matter of time until your slice of the pie becomes so small that your business is no longer viable.

Even if you are the market leader, it's good to keep an eye on your market share. Knowing that you have a dominant share of the market may be a competitive advantage to leverage while negotiating loans, prices, or exploring new product categories. Conversely, a limited market share may cause you to focus on niche areas, differentiation strategies, or market penetration tactics to gain a stronger foothold. In either scenario, understanding your market share provides essential insights for making basic strategic decisions.

In addition to gauging the health of your own business, you can also use the intelligence you gained by doing market share calculations to determine if your market is expanding or contracting. Growing markets are more attractive investment targets than markets in contraction.

Understanding market share can also identify your competitors who are leaders in your market. While you'll never get ahead by outright copying what another business is doing, you may have something to learn by closely examining how they make decisions. (The book is named *Spying on Success* for a reason.)

In Las Vegas, where I live, the impact of large events can be difficult to gauge because profits are closely held secrets by those that compete for that money. So when the Super Bowl or Formula One racing comes to town, the value of the event is often determined by monitoring the artifacts surrounding the event. Some examples include: hotel occupancy rates, water or sewer use, collected taxes, ride-share wait times, crime rates, and emergency hospital visits.

Market share typically is a measure of sales, but any business process metric (input or output) can be substituted. Calculating market share with non-sales totals can often reveal a diverse set of intelligence. Here are a few alternatives to gross sales that can be used to indicate market share.

- The amount of resources consumed
- The amount of waste generated
- The number of satisfied customers

- Percentage of employees retained
- Any mandated reporting
- Total money invested in research and development.

Nearly any organizational input or output may be used to gauge total market performance.

Your industry may have particularly rich and available sources.

Objective: Improve procurement

Competitive intelligence can play a critical role in procurement by identifying when markets, or individual items, are worth buying. The more volatile the market, the bigger impact competitive intelligence may have.

It is not difficult to set up a competitive intelligence campaign to monitor a vendor and alert you when there's a buying opportunity caused by a favorable change in an item's: description, terms, or price. It's not that much harder to have that same bot buy the item before anyone else sees it.

Once a system like this is established, one can analyze the quantity of items purchased at or below the target price. If this number of items available at the preferred price is decreasing, the campaign should trigger an **alert** that a supply problem may be in development.

Additionally, competitive intelligence allows procurement teams to benchmark supplier performance against industry standards and identify areas for improvement.

Objective: Gauging the preferences of customers

Competitive intelligence allows businesses to gain a better understanding of customer satisfaction. By understanding customers' preferences, pain points, and perceptions of competing offerings, companies can gain valuable insights into market trends and customer needs.

41

The most common way to gauge customer preferences is through surveys, which are covered in detail in *Chapter 10, Finding Sources*. While well designed surveys gather specific data, don't forget to look at the *metadata,* or the context for the data contained within the survey. Some of the unintended communication from surveys include:

- What was the percentage of competed surveys?
- How many partially competed surveys were there?
- How many people only responded to one question?
- Were the completed surveys all collected from the same location?
- Are there indications that some respondents submitted more than one survey?
- Was there an even distribution of responses over the duration of the survey, or were they all submitted at once?
- Are any metrics trending in any particular direction?

Today artificial intelligence can evaluate text (and maybe by the time you read this, audio too?) to determine customer mood, engagement, or satisfaction. AI can then convert the mood of text into numeric information can displayed with gauges on executive dashboards.

Objective: Improve employee recruitment

competitive intelligence provides opportunities to learn about the talent pool before you need to look for applicants. For example, a competitive intelligence campaign could be devised to monitor LinkedIn to find the top performers in your industry. This campaign could develop a database of the players in your field, as well as their employment status and responsibilities. A competitive intelligence campaign could use this data to statistically calculate which employees are most likely to be looking for new employment and be easiest to recruit. Such a list would provide a strategic competitive advantage for an organization or a recruiting company. Such actionable intelligence could certainly drive down the cost, and raise the effectiveness, of recruiting campaigns.

Objective: Become instant experts

There are many reasons why an organization might need to gain expertise in a short amount of time, ranging from making an acquisition to exploring a new opportunity. Competitive intelligence can help bring expertise into an organization through automated data collection, analysis, and targeted notifications.

I once had a client that was studying the emerging cannabis industry here in the United States. They commissioned a custom web spider that looked for new articles relating to the industry. These articles were arranged in a library (a searchable database) where information could be easily accessed.

You might be asking how this is more effective than just using Google. Here are some of the benefits of such a system:

- The data can be personalized and filtered to show specifically what the client is looking for.

- A custom spider can examine anything on The Internet, and not just what is indexed by Google.

- When you collect the data, you know the exact source and how old the data is.

- You can observe if stories are edited or deleted after publication.

- You can generate alerts, in the form of text messages or emails, when important events occur.

- A custom system can normalize the data, so you're not always seeing the same material in different places.

- One can see how quickly ideas and trends spread.

43

- Artificial intelligence can be applied to compare and contrast found articles.

- You can also use artificial intelligence and be used to gauge emotional qualities of an article. Without AI, it is very difficult to automate and gauge the detection of: cautious, optimistic, humorous, altering, or irrelevant information.

- Custom collection software isn't reliant on Google's spider schedules and can run as often as needed.

- Google can't access information behind firewalls or websites you pay to access.

- The data collected by custom search agents can be more easily integrated into in-house systems.

Plus, there's a general competitive intelligence principle that says: Google shows you what everyone else sees, while a custom agent shows you what no one else is watching.

Objective: Be the first-to-know

One of the more common requests is for an organization to be notified as soon as an event happens. You may want advance warning of include when:

- A price changes.

- Items can be procured at desirable terms.

- Your competitors file new patents, court records, mortgages, or building permits.

- Your organization, a supplier, or a customer, is mentioned in the news.

- There are potential disruptions caused by weather, market conditions, supply chains, or funding issues.

- You have new competitors with competing products.

Competitive intelligence campaigns that ensure that the client is first to know about something are interesting to develop because they cover a broad span of potential targets.

Objective: Reduce time-to-action

If your objective is to be first to know something is happening, the next logical step is to be first to act. If your campaign uses automation to find the intelligence, it should also be able to: buy, sell, trade, or literally move on intelligence as soon as it's discovered. These campaigns address a major problem with organizations, especially large ones; that being reducing the time to action.

Objective: To avoid surprises

Competitive intelligence empowers organizations to anticipate the future by providing actionable insights into competitor activities and industry trends. By systematically collecting intelligence from industry reports, government records, market research studies, news articles, and social media, organizations can build a history of activity that can be analyzed and trends can be detected. Here again, artificial intelligence can be employed to help summarize and detect trends. In that regard, competitive intelligence is the closest you'll get to predicting the future.

Objective: Discover competitor's strategies

Knowing your competitor's business strategies creates many compare and contrast opportunities; the tasks that artificial intelligence excels at. Now that so much business is conducted online, the thumbprint left by business is larger and easier to access. It becomes fairly easy to observe your competitor and *Reverse Engineer* what they're doing.

The following show a few of your competitor's business strategies that can be observed by simple internet monitoring and analysis.

Strategy	Approach
Search Optimization	You learn insights into your competitor's web strategy by analyzing their webpage's meta tags, content, and link strategy. You can measure their success by monitoring where they appear in web searches.
Advertising strategies	Similarly to search optimization, you can monitor your competitors online advertising to reveal the keywords they thought were worth buying, and what they paid for them.
Retail strategies	By monitoring which products your competitor sells, and when inventory falls short, you can tell a lot about competing organization's retail and inventory strategy.
Fulfillment strategies	The story in the preface showed how important fulfillment strategies are; given the lengths that Modell's was willing to go to collect it from their competitor. Fortunately, retail strategies are pretty transparent and revealed when your competitors fulfill orders.

Using competitive intelligence to observe competitor strategies

Objective: Predicting competitor behavior

Anticipating competitors' likely responses to market changes, industry disruptions can help you prepare for your own future. Monitoring both your markets and your competitor's organizational inputs and outputs provides intelligence to recognize both trends and inevitabilities.

Competitors become predictable when you are able to anticipate their reactions to changes in their environment. And once they become predictable, they can be manipulated. There is an example of an online store that was able to control their competitors prices. in *Chapter 6: Monitoring systems.*

Objective: Identifying acquisition targets

Competitive intelligence offers unique opportunities to identify potential collaboration opportunities, partnerships, or acquisition targets. Once a competitive market is understood, it's easy to pick-out the underperforming businesses in strong markets. These findings may identify acquisition targets that could be turned around with better management.

Objective: Protect intellectual property

A partner and I were once approached by a law firm with the following problem. They represented a teen female celebrity, whose likeness was used online without authorization. The fact that she was underage, and that the images were often photoshopped and sexual in nature, created an immediate need to protect her personal brand.

In this particular campaign, there needed to be a way to manage the identification and removal of these images. The harsh reality, however, is that there is not a lot of accountability on the Internet. So getting people to remove content can be difficult. It is important, however, to document that a removal request was made and to monitor if, or when, the offending content was removed. In other words, the campaign had to work within the limits of the medium.

The proposed solution aimed to:

- Identify where and when offending images were found.
- Log the offending content.
- Identify domain owners
- Make a formal (automated) request for the removal of the offending content.
- Create a paper trail of descriptions of the images, when and where they were found, when the domain owner was contacted, what was said to them, and a record of the website owner's response.

This is also a good example of a campaign that benefited from automation as searching the entire Internet for specific images

47

would be very time consuming, especially if the searches were done on an ongoing basis.

Courts like to see the owners of intellectual property protect their content. This campaign's objective wasn't to automatically remove offending images. The objective was to satisfy court requirements if further prosecution was required.

Another problem is when a trademark becomes so popular that it becomes the generic name for something through a process known as *genericide*. The original owners of trademarks like: Vaseline, Kleenex, Aspirin, Heroin, Escalator, Zipper, and Cellophane lost exclusive use to those trademarks because they didn't actively defend their trademarks against generic use. A competitive intelligence campaign could be developed with the objective of detecting generic use of your trademarks.

Conducting a needs-based audit

The first part of this chapter reviewed a few business objectives that easily align with the capabilities of competitive intelligence. The rest of this chapter is dedicated to those organizations, where needs are not as easily identified or matched to competitive intelligence capabilities. In those cases a needs based audit is required.

Law of the Minimum

Needs are closely tied to deficiencies. Most organizations typically do their best to hide their problems. So if you're having difficulty detecting the hidden needs or deficiencies in your organization, consider using the *Law of the minimum*.

"The law of the Minimum" is credited to Justus Von Liebig, a 19th century German scientist, who is primarily remembered as the person who developed chemical fertilizers. In the process of feeding the world, he came-up with this rule:

"If one essential nutrient is missing, growth

will be difficult, even when all other
nutrients are abundant."

This principle is obviously applied to agriculture, but it has also been applied to business. The Law of the Minimum underscores the importance of identifying and addressing the most limiting factors in a system. Finding those limiting factors often points toward solutions that can be afforded by competitive intelligence.

One of the best ways to find the deficiencies in a business is to create a process flow diagram. An example of a generic process flow is shown below.

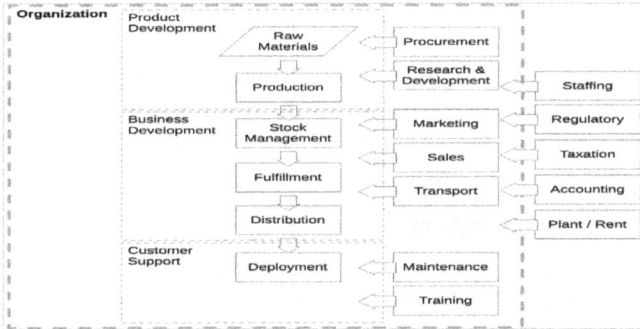

Generic organizational process flow

A process flow diagram provides a guide to show the interactions between inputs and outputs. Any organization should be able to develop a process flow diagram similar to the example above, regardless of what is being manufactured or serviced. In fact, you could deep-dive and create something similar for each product line, location, or service offered.

For example, if your organization sells household appliances, you may want to perform this process for each aspect of your business, like:

- New appliance sales
- Used appliance sales
- Labor, maintenance and repairs
- Waste removal
- Sales of accessories.

Once you've identified your processes and interactions between processes, apply the Law of the Minimum to find the choke points. Those process bottlenecks are the generators of potential competitive intelligence objectives.

It's a good idea to get as many perspectives on your needs-based audit as possible. This is the one place, and as you'll learn perhaps the only place, where you'll want a lot of opinions on a campaign.

Further thoughts

There's no way to underplay the importance of planning and documenting your objectives. The next chapter describes techniques for documenting your campaign in a playbook.

Chapter 3: Setting objectives

Spying on Success

C hapter 4

Creating a playbook

The playbook is the documentation that describes your campaign's objectives, tactics, and sources.

Documentation is not merely a formality; it is a crucial preparatory step for a successful competitive intelligence campaign. The playbook for your campaign offers a platform for strategic planning and helps prevent potential oversights that might not be as apparent in a campaign without documentation.

Symptoms of under-planning

It cannot be overstated how important planning is. Perhaps the best way to emphasize the importance of planning is to understand the symptoms of under-planning.

Use QR code to access video, "The Symptoms of Under-planning"

Symptom: Data for the sake of data

Many competitive intelligence campaigns exist solely to collect data, with no real plan for what to do with the data once is it collected.

In the last chapter, you read about the importance of identifying your campaign's objective. As obvious as that sounds, many competitive intelligence campaigns exist solely to collect data, with no real plan for what to do with the data once it is collected.

While there is expense involved in maintaining such campaigns, the real expense comes when people create undocumented uses for the data. Over time, it's easy to acquire volumes of reports generated from the data, again without documentation. As people come and go, eventually organizations find themselves relying on reports that no one is responsible for. And when the reports stop working, no one will know how to fix them.

Symptom: Feature creep

Feature creep is the unplanned expansion of product features, often triggered by technology. Over time it leads to bloated, overly complex systems that are difficult to use or maintain.

The other prime source of feature creep comes from stakeholders, who don't fully understand the impact of last minute suggestions. In my experience, feature creep requests are most apt to happen after a missed deadline.

Case study: Rite Aid

What could have been a beneficial use of artificial intelligence became a nightmare for the US retail pharmacy, Rite Aid. They successfully defined an objective, and a tactic for collecting the needed data, but things deteriorated rapidly when they later added artificial intelligence features that were outside of the original project scope.

Rite Aid's objective was to secure stores that are open twenty-four hours a day and seven days a week. This problem has been made more acute by the growing shortage of people willing to work late night and early morning hours for traditionally low wages. Solving this problem would give Rite Aid a clear competitive advantage.

Initially, the strategy was to use surveillance cameras to provide both a security presence and as a way to collect video evidence, should it be required. This seemed like a sound idea. But they soon realized that their strategy neither protected their staff nor deterred theft. So they decided to add a facial recognition feature to the strategy. Once set-up, the new surveillance system could automatically identify known criminals as they enter the store.

This surveillance system, with facial recognition, sounded very useful. But it also created a new problem. What should employees do if an actual criminal *did* enter the store?

Only after it was installed did Rite Aid realize the limitations of the new security features. So they did what any pressured management team would do: *they added more features*. This time they lowered the threshold to include "potential shoplifters" or just "troublemakers".

As you may expect, this security campaign was a disaster. But regardless of the poor track record, they ran the campaign for eight years. During this period, the program generated thousands of false reports.

According to the cited article, this AI generated intelligence was used as an excuse to stop and accuse innocent shoppers of crimes, often in front of their friends and family.[9] The system's artificial intelligence also held a bias toward flagging women

---

[9]   Gibson, K. (2023, December 20). *Rite aid's "covert surveillance program" falsely id'd customers as shoplifters, FTC says.* CBS News. https://www.cbsnews.com/news/ai-rite-aid-customers-falsely-identified-as-shoplifters-ftc/

and people of color. Additionally, these systems stored massive amounts of personally identifying information that is otherwise regulated for the public's safety.

As a result of this poorly planned campaign, the US Federal Trade Commission banned Rite Aid from using artificial intelligence for a period of five years[10]. To their credit, Rite Aid voluntarily discontinued the campaign before the FTC began investigating. By the spring of 2025, Rite Aid had filed for their second bankruptcy protection. And by that October, they closed all remaining stores. While there were several events that contributed to their demise, the lawsuits spawned from feature creep didn't help their case,

Symptom: Over-sampling

It doesn't matter if your are working in the physical or online world, you need to treat sources with the upmost respect. And the easiest way to disrespect a source is to contact it too often. As competitive intelligence moved online, this over use of sources became known as over-sampling. Your goal should be to contact source servers only as much as need to to get the data you need, and no more.

There are two reasons for showing sources so much respect:

- If you contact a source too often, you can jeopardize the reliability of the source. This would be difficult to do in the physical world; but with computers, online sources, and automation, it's quite easy to get too aggressive.

- If you generate too much traffic, you will gain attention to yourself. And once a source realizes that it is a source, it may implement countermeasures that

---

[10] Roth, E. (2023, December 20). *Rite Aid hit with five-year facial recognition ban over reckless use*. The Verge. https://www.theverge.com/2023/12/19/24008516/rite-aid-facial-recognition-ban-ftc-five-years

threaten the existence of your campaign.

Sometimes I'm amazed at people's disregard for sources. For example, I was once asked to develop what I thought was a simple price monitoring campaign for an online store.

The proposal called for monitoring nearly a million products. That's a lot of products to monitor, but it's not impossible, depending on the sampling rate. But this client wanted the prices, for the entire store, checked every five seconds. Obviously, to update several million products that often would require that my bots hit the servers several million times a second. At that point, our intelligence campaign would clearly make the source website the most trafficked site on the Internet and there would be no way to hide our presence.

Even when presented with these facts, the client insisted on over-sampling the source. So I turned down the project.

Oversampling is one of the reasons I don't normally use artificial intelligence for sourcing data, especially in fully automated systems. In addition to the unknown quality of the data, you have absolutely no control over how many times your artificial intelligence engine touches the source or what it leaves in their access logs.

Symptom: Losing anonymity

Anonymity makes it easier for organizations to operate online. Even when you are sourcing intelligence from public sources, you still want to maintain anonymity for the simple reason that anonymity helps ensure the privacy of your organization. This privacy is important because competitive intelligence campaigns are run in hopes of providing a competitive advantage. Obviously, if you jeopardize your anonymity, you also jeopardize your campaign and the trade secret you hope it becomes.

One might counter and say, *"If you have nothing to hide, why are you trying to be anonymous?"*

To that I would counter that one may have nothing to hide, but still want to close their curtains from time to time.

When subscription-based websites are used as sources, you trade your identity for access. In these situations, your bots should not only refrain from over sampling, but also exhibit human-like traits, for example: operating at a human (not computer) rate, avoiding redundant actions, occasionally waiting random amounts of time, and accessing data during regular business hours.

Symptom: Ignored automation opportunities

Failing to automate is perhaps more accurately a symptom of competitive intelligence campaigns that don't get off the ground. The vast majority of the campaigns I've worked on could only be practically performed by computers.

Employing people to perform intelligence collection is expensive and error prone. If you plan on collecting data from the same place more than once, you should also plan to automate it.

Symptom: Unethical behavior

Another symptom of poor planning in competitive intelligence Campaigns is the collapse of ethics.

At this point, it might be good to remind ourselves that unethical behavior is seldom planned. Instead, unethical decisions usually happen in a vacuum and without a written code of ethics in their playbook.

Perhaps one of the more unethical competitive intelligence campaigns has become known as *The Dirty Tricks Scandal.* The Dirty Tricks Scandal stemmed from *British Airways'* frustrations with emerging competition, *Virgin Airlines*[11].

Richard Branson's upstart airline had been eating into British Airways' profits and prestige. The final blow may have occurred when Virgin Airlines rescued British citizens from Kuwait just prior to the *Gulf War*. British Airways had always been the default airline of the United Kingdom. So not only was Virgin a threat to their bottom line, British Airways' pride was also hurt. "Something had to be done with *Branson!*"[12]

Part of British Airways strategy was to leverage another asset they owned, a booking system called *BABS,* or *British Airways Booking System*. BABS wasn't just the booking system used by British Airways; it was also used by all the regional airlines, travel agents, and airports across Europe. It just happened that BABS was owned by British Airways.

In addition to data related to flight reservations, BABS also maintained a trip status and knew when flights were cancelled or delayed.

During this period, British Airways also employed a team of people called the Helpline. Members of the Helpline met arriving passengers and assisted with flight connections and transfers. Helpline employees needed access to BABS data to do their jobs. BABS gave them access to: flight manifests including passenger names and phone numbers, the nature of delays, and other privileged data.

The Dirty Tricks Scandal first encouraged Helpline members to use privileged BABS data to poach travelers flying on Virgin Airlines. They instructed the Helpline to meet passengers

---

[11] Independent Digital News and Media. (1993, January 12). *Battle of the airlines: How the dirty tricks campaign was run: Martyn*. The Independent. https://www.independent.co.uk/news/uk/battle-of-the-airlines-how-the-dirty-tricks-campaign-was-run-martyn-gregory-reports-on-ba-s-dirty-tricks-campaign-which-he-uncovered-as-producer-director-of-thames-television-s-this-week-programme-1478010.html

[12] *ibid*

coming off delayed flights and offer easy transfers to British Airways. Sometimes they would use BABS to acquire personal phone numbers which BA would use to contact passengers directly. Additionally, British Airways employees learned they could pose as Virgin employees and call the baggage handlers to get even more information needed to steal passengers.

The Dirty Tricks Scandal had disastrous effects on Virgin Airlines. According to Richard Branson, if they had only the airline, Virgin would have "gone down". Richard Branson also exclaimed that if this had happened in America, people would be sent to prison for fraudulent behavior[13].

A lack of ethics, unclear objectives, feature creep, over-sampling, losing anonymity, and missing opportunities are only a few symptoms of poorly planned competitive intelligence campaigns. But hopefully this list is long enough to pique your awareness to recognize such planning mistakes.

What is the objective?

One clear way to help avoid ethical problems is to clearly define the business objective of your campaign. Your objective is the specific business problem your campaign will solve, or new opportunity it will afford.

To best define your objective, try saying something like,

> *"What competitive advantage can competitive intelligence provide that will help me (state your objective here)".*

Over my career, I have inherited a number of competitive intelligence campaigns that had absolutely no objective other

---

13   Independent Digital News and Media. (1993, January 12). *Battle of the airlines: How the dirty tricks campaign was run: Martyn*. The Independent. https://www.independent.co.uk/news/uk/battle-of-the-airlines-how-the-dirty-tricks-campaign-was-run-martyn-gregory-reports-on-ba-s-dirty-tricks-campaign-which-he-uncovered-as-producer-director-of-thames-television-s-this-week-programme-1478010.html

than to collect data (in case it was needed someday). Without written direction or scope, these campaigns change focus as often as they change hands. The result are massive systems of which maybe only 5% is used, but 100% needs to be maintained. It's very difficult to turn these systems off because of all the undocumented interconnectivity. All of these problems can be avoided by declaring and committing to the campaign's objective.

Who is the customer?

A common business axiom is to *"know your customer"*. This phrase is often applied to retail customers, but it also refers to internal customers as well. It's vital to identify the end customer of your competitive intelligence campaign because ultimately, the customer determines the content and format of your deliverables.

Deliverables

The final product of your competitive intelligence campaign can take two basic forms:

- The intelligence is delivered in the form of analysis, where the raw data is also available for transparency. This analysis can take the format of informative spreadsheets, charts, dashboards, or videos.

- When the intelligence is inherently actionable, or an immediate action is required to capture a competitive advantage, the system that collected the intelligence should also take immediate action. In these cases, a human may be notified that an action took place, but the call-to-action is automatically triggered by the campaign's analysis.

Determine your ROI

Before you determine a budget for your campaign, you need to consider the financial return on your investment.

In some cases, like in preparation for an acquisition, your budgets are set by your own needs for due diligence. But in other cases, you might want to calculate potential returns before deploying your campaign. For example, how important would it be to find out the online ad strategy for your most successful competitor? It probably depends on how badly they're beating you and how important advertising is to your own organization.

It is highly recommended, when possible, to build ROI calculation directly into the reporting functions. You're doing all that analysis anyway, you may as well include ROI too. I learned this lesson after failing to measure the value of the inventory procured by a very successful automated procurement system. That campaign purchased several tens of millions of dollars in highly valued inventory over a short period of time. If I had recorded the value of the inventory purchased, it would have been easier to demonstrate the value of the campaign.

Project lifecycles

As a rule, senior management doesn't like open-ended projects. So your playbook should document your campaign's planned termination, or succession. Here are some questions that your campaign lifecycle planning should answer.

- Is this a campaign that is run once, or will it be periodic?
- Which existing process is this campaign replacing?
- How long will it take before this campaign is operational?
- How will we know that the campaign is over?
- What calamities may cause this project to be delayed or cancelled?
- What is the expected lifecycle of the sources?

It's common for intelligence sources to dry-up as quickly as they are discovered. So, be aware that the lifecycle of your campaign may be dictated by the availability of your sources. For this reason, it's preferred to also have backup and alternate sources in case your primary sources go away.

List your challenges

As all competitive intelligence campaigns have challenges. It's best to identify them in your playbook and plan to plan accordingly, before you begin.

DevOps

If your campaign is automated with software, your campaign becomes a software development project. So it will need procedures for back-ups, deployment, and maintenance. These procedures should be in your playbook

Looking human

Another challenge to consider if you automate a campaign, and sometimes if you don't, is the need to conduct your campaign without drawing attention to yourself.

Left unchecked, automated software programs tend to act very differently than people performing the same task. This is because software (and software developers) look for opportunities to improve speed and efficiency.

Competitive intelligence campaigns, however, are one place where you don't want to be efficient. You want your software to run with all of the inefficiencies that a person would exhibit.

Sometimes the solution is to make one bot look like a team of people. Other times, you throttle data collection speeds down to something that won't raise eyebrows.

It's important to calculate the amount of data that needs to be collected and the time required to collect it. If you need more time, you need to take it. You simply can't allow your data collection to over-access the source server. Failure to take these precautions will make you look conspicuous.

Disaster planning

Something that could affect your campaign's lifecycle are unexpected changes to its operating environment. It's best to plan for these situations before they happen. Some simple disaster planning is identified below.

Disaster	Consequences	Mediation
You lose your main source (website).	The campaign is lost if you don't have alternative sources selected.	Pre-select alternative sources.
Your campaign is discovered.	You have to deal with the lose of the campaign and potential embarrassment.	Do everything possible to maintain anonymity and plausible deniability. Prepare what to say to the source if asked.
Your source developed countermeasures	You may be blocked from the source (website), need to find a new source, or you just lost a trade secret that provided a competitive advantage.	Treat your source as kindly as possible. If the source is lost, it's not because of your campaign.

Playbook disaster planning

A lot of the disasters listed above can be avoided if you treat your sources as kindly as possible. This means you don't over sample or otherwise bring attention to yourself from using an overly aggressive tactic.

Disaster planning: example

Knowing how you'll respond to disaster before it happens takes the emotion out of your decision making process, if or when the disaster does happen.

There was one particular campaign, early in my career, where I developed a bot to monitor a website. Apparently, my bot was overly aggressive and connected to the website too often. In all honesty, I knew I was making a mistake in running the bot too fast. But I compromised and let the client, who wanted better performance, to influence my better sensibilities.

One afternoon my CEO client asked me to join him on a phone conversation. Once connected I heard him say, "Hey Mike, someone wants to talk to you."

The person on the other end of the conversation was the IT manager of the website we were using as a source. He wanted to know why we were accessing the website so often. Fortunately, I had planned for this conversation, because I was personally uncomfortable with how often we were downloading their website. A lot of my planning was centered on telling the source how important they were.

This could have been a tense situation. But I came prepared. After taking a deep breath, I simply explained that we did a lot of business on their website (we did) and that we were in the process of finding new ways to do even more business with them (we were). I apologized for the misunderstanding and promised to be less aggressive and looked forward to an even closer business relationship, now that we personally knew each other.

Having been in that IT manager's position, I knew that this would be an easy conclusion to an otherwise awkward phone call. His conversation when from confronting a suspected hacker to discovering that they had a customer that was looking for new ways to engage. I learned from this experience and never received a similar phone call since.

Tactics and sources

Your tactics are how you plan to achieve your objective from the intelligence available at your sources. There are universal considerations that apply to all tactics, as shown on the next page.

Many of these considerations are an extension of disaster planning.

Consideration	Rational
Will you be performing the campaign manually or through automation?	Manual campaigns are great for testing concepts. But, you should always look for opportunities to drive costs down and improve performance through automation.
If you need to log into a source, how will you protect your anonymity?	You may meet counterintelligence or be blocked if the source feels you're trying to achieve a competitive advantage and they need to protect their other users.
How can you run the campaign and not become obvious?	Again, this is a matter of tuning your tactics to only touch the source as little as possible.
How long will the source be available?	I've worked on several campaigns that capitalized on a website's flaw. These flaws, however, are eventually fixed, signaling the end of the campaign. Knowing this adds an extra sense of urgency to the campaign.
Is the data hard to harvest?	Tactics that are difficult to deploy almost always ensure that the client has a monopoly on this data, which hopefully also translates into a monopoly on a competitive advantage.

Tactic and source considerations

Scarcity and difficulty are your friends

You don't need to identify your data sources before you start planning your tactics, but this is usually one of the first steps.

Generally speaking, your best data sources are those that are:

- Proprietary
- Hard to capture or
- Captured from multiple sources.

When useful intelligence is difficult to gather it automatically becomes more valuable. The one who has the data has a monopoly on it's use.

There have been several projects in my past that we actually had to scale back our efforts to hide the fact that we had created a substantial competitive advantage.

While the emphasis of modern competitive intelligence relies primarily on online sources, this is also a good time to explore if any offline data can also be used.

Technology choices

Your tactics may require some technology and possibly custom access and screen scraping software.

When the web was young, there were many ways to download websites. Today, with the increased use of *active content*, and other immersive technologies, there are basically two paths the technology in your campaigns can take:

- Since there is so much dynamic content, generated by javascript, some developers take a direct JavaScript approach and use a JavaScript-derived technology like Node.js[14].

- My preference is to use a more stable and versatile platform, like Selenium. Selenium is an interface into a variety of browsers, where it allows for full control with the comfort of more conventional languages like Python, Java, or PHP. Selenium is also more scalable than a JavaScript solution.

Identify the call to action

There needs to be something of consequence to do after analysis otherwise theres no need for your competitive intelligence campaign. This is your call to action. Your call to action may be small, like changing a price, or it could be momentous, like deciding to buy a competitor.

Actionable intelligence is important, even in cases where the

---

[14]   https://nodejs.org

object of the campaign is situational awareness. There needs to be something in that sea of data that is important enough for an action to be taken, or there's no real need for the campaign.

Keep written ethical guidelines

If ethics aren't planned, failures will ensue. So it's advisable to have a defined set of ethical standards. These considerations don't have to be extremely detailed. For example, Google's old mantra of, *"Do no evil"*, works. It's succinct and absolute.

You can boil most competitive intelligence ethics into the following:

1. Don't touch your sources any more than absolutely necessary.

2. Do not create any campaign that keeps someone else from accessing their own resources.

3. Observe industry regulations.

If professionalism doesn't sway you into making ethical choices, consider your personal embarrassment when you're forced into telling your boss or client that the multimillion dollar competitive intelligence campaign, that you're responsible for, was prematurely terminated because you got caught doing something sketchy. It will likely be the last competitive intelligence campaign you do for them.

Further thoughts

A wonderful way to incorporate artificial intelligence into your competitive intelligence campaigns is to ask it to critique your playbook. Ask it about strengths, weaknesses, and potential return on investment.

Spying on Success: Tactics

C hapter 5
Approaching tactics

In years past, competitive intelligence was mostly conducted through reading publications, attending conferences, or having direct contact with the target of the investigation. But then the '90s happened and competitive intelligence was handed its greatest gift, The Internet.

This chapter offers tactics for best approaching online intelligence sources. Many of these techniques can also be applied to physical intelligence sources as well. But they probably won't benefit from any of the three elements of online intelligence gathering. Those being: Anonymity, Remoteness, and Automation.

Don't be part of the intended audience

Some of the best intelligence is that which is communicated unintentionally. And the best way to find unintentionally communicated intelligence is by distancing yourself from the habits and concerns of the target audience. Becoming someone other than the intended audience facilitates discovering cases of both over-communication and unintended communication.

Hear the unsaid

Hearing the unsaid, or unintentionally said, sounds important. But how is it done? In order to hear messages that are indirectly communicated, it's good to remember the OPSEC question asked earlier.

"What could an adversary learn about us

just by observing our operation?"

Advertisements, especially online ads, are one of the better sources of intelligence. Obviously, advertisements and sales catalogs, are excellent places to find product and pricing information. But platforms and businesses often over-communicate and reveal more about themselves than they intended. As investigators, separating ourselves from the typical buying public is our ticket to reading some of this unintended communication.

For example, let's explore the advertisement below. This ad could appear anywhere. But for now, let's assume it's a advertisement on an online marketplace like eBay.

Black Foldable Travel Umbrella

Best Travel eCommerce Deals Inc (5312)
98.6% positive · Seller's other items · Contact seller

US $34.95/ea

Condition: **New**

Quantity: [1] 24 available

Sample eBay posting

The figure above shows a posting for a black travel umbrella with a buy-it-now price of $34.95. But if you look around, you can usually find other, less obvious, contributing information as well.

An investigator may assume that this item is a slow seller. We can deduce this because we're told that there are twenty-four items available. This number, two dozen, would be an unusually precise quantity for an item that sells quickly. But it's easy to see how umbrellas may be wholesaled by the dozen.

The other, less plausible, reason to see a stock of two dozen is that that we just happened to come across this posting after they restocked.

If we watch this posting periodically, we'll start to notice that the inventory quantity decrements with each item sold. So if we divide sample period by the change in inventory, we can determine how many umbrellas this seller sells per day[15]. If on Monday there are twenty-four available, and only sixteen available on Wednesday, that evidence tells us that they sold eight umbrellas in two days.

So in addition to saying, "I have a Black Foldable Travel Umbrella for sale at $34.95", the seller is also inadvertently providing evidence to indicate:

- The product's rate of sale
- The number of days until the inventory needs to be replenished
- The seasonality of the sales
- The quantity of units the seller buys at a time
- If the demand is increasing or decreasing.

While we're at it, why not extend this investigation to include the other items the seller sells in their eBay store. While expanding our scope, we can also learn:

- What are this seller's fastest selling products?
- Which of the seller's products sell most slowly?
- Is the business growing or contracting?
- Is there a pattern in item updates? If so, it's evident that those items may be procured from the same source.
- What their warehousing needs are, based on product

---

[15] Yes, it's a little more complicated than that, because the inventory level can also increase. When this happens restart the clock and to start analyzing the next set of data.

dimensions and combined sales rates for all products?

- What is the average rate of sales for all their products, and indirectly, their gross sales?

Additionally, through the gift of automation, we could also perform the analysis on all of this eBay seller's competitors. With this information we could not only obtain market share information, but we could look for statistical anomalies to identify hot products that haven't been noticed by other sellers.

The reality is that a simple list of products, ranked by profitability, would be an incredible competitive advantage to anyone looking at setting-up a similar eBay store.

Further thoughts

This chapter emphasized that sometimes unintentional communication is easier to detect when you're not part of the intended audience.

Sometimes, however, it's hard *not to be* part of the intended audience; especially when the website is well designed. If you fall into this situation, you might find that you're better able to maintain your objectivity if you role play that you're someone else. Pretend that you're not a fan of the content, but perhaps a reviewer or critic of some kind.

The reason behind all this suggested role-play is to help the investigator identify and remove themselves from their own personal biases.

C hapter 6
Monitoring systems

There are a number of things that competitive intelligence does exceptionally well, like monitoring competitive environments. This chapter explores the various types of monitoring tactics, including:

- First-to-know tactics
- Notification systems
- Automated calls to action
- Price intelligence
- Procurement tools
- Situational awareness.

As you will learn, monitoring is more than merely watching.

First-to-know tactics

One of the main reasons to monitor a situation is to be the first to know when something of importance happens. In my experience, these campaigns are usually procurement systems announcing the availability of prime inventory.

And good example of this type of tactic was a campaign I worked on after the last real estate collapse. The client wanted to develop an active database of foreclosed homes. In addition to collecting a database of these homes, where statistical analysis could be performed, he also wanted to be the first to know when new foreclosed properties were added so he could be the first to act on opportunities.

The thing to remember in these campaigns is that the tools to detect these events can also act on these opportunities.

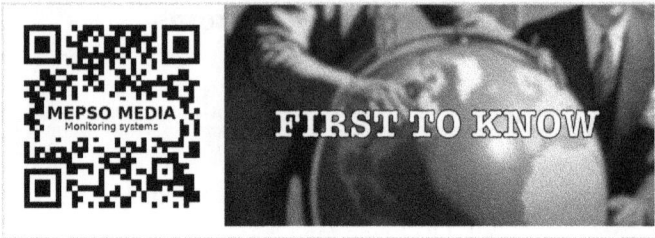

Use QR code to access video, "Monitoring Systems"

Notification systems

If the website you're monitoring finds information of immediate importance, you'll need a notification system.

Notifications can take many forms. When portability and immediacy are important, notifications sent as text messages are hard to beat.

Alert systems are an area where CI developers can get creative. For example, your campaign could send alerts to a special account on *Twitter, (*now *X)*. As odd as it sounds, this could be a great notification platform in some cases because it restricts those who get the notifications, plus you can use the platform's *OTT*, or Over the Top protocols to produce notifications on cellphones, tablets, etc. Additionally, all the notifications become archived for later study.

When I know that the client will be within earshot of their computer, I prefer to create a website that is left open in a browser that monitors the campaign, writes status messages, and makes audible alerts.

Notifications systems are fun because it's one of the few times the competitive intelligence consultant gets to interface directly with clients. In one case, I developed a campaign that used the bark of a small dog to notify a client when something of interest appeared at auction. The friendly bark of a dog was a good choice because the sound was out of character for his office and got immediate attention. The dog would only bark when an auctioned item met a set of prequalified conditions for: price, description, and condition. The qualifications ensured that the dog didn't bark too often. That is important because notifications that are sent too often quickly become annoyances.

Monitoring campaigns are capable of monitoring more than one thing at a time. Your tactic may require that you look for a combination of events that exist simultaneously. If your campaign is monitoring multiple events it's best to choose alerts with unique sounds to indicate when various conditions are met. Audible alerts also allow the campaign to run while you're doing something else. You only need to look up when you hear a sound you're anticipating.

Automated calls to action

The systems that monitor and find actionable intelligence are usually also capable of acting on that intelligence. For example, if a bot looks for the availability of a specific product at a specific price, why shouldn't the same software that discovered the opportunity also buy the product when it finds it?

Systems that make automated purchases can scare people. But when sufficient safeguards are in place, like capping your daily spend and the quantity of daily buys, these projects can be highly rewarding.

Calls to action that are easily automated include:

- Purchases, when items are available at preferred price and terms

- Sales, when qualified offers are received

- Bank transfers, when funds need to be replenished

79

- Group announcements, when large communications are warranted

- Holds on other systems, when external factors influence internal business.

Notifications can be routine or exceptional. Nearly any source or metric can be set-up on a notification system.

Library campaigns

Another form of monitoring campaign is one that searches for and compiles a library of information. Library campaigns automatically find information on a specific subject, make it accessible to researchers, and develop notifications, or other calls-to-action, that fit predefined filters. Such tactics increase institutional knowledge and make that knowledge immediately available either internally or to others on a subscription basis.

Investors use library campaigns to quickly gain expertise in emerging commodities markets. In my experience, the smaller the niche the more value this intelligence has.

These campaigns typically employ web spiders that are seeded with an initial list of URLs. As the spider runs more URLs are found and added to the list. As the links to the URLs are explored, the content is matched to a set of keywords that determine if the page has meaningful information. If relevant content is found, it is harvested, timestamped, metadata is created, and everything is sent to a database for later analysis.

Keyword matching

The object of many campaigns is to find specific keywords on monitored webpages. These keywords are landmarks that one would expect to find on webpages with relevant content. In addition to locating relevant information, keywords can also become a source of metadata by tracking where and how often keywords appear.

Keywords can also have hierarchy. For example, your highest level keyword might be "Lithium". But you may also have location keywords like: "California", "Nevada" and "Chile". Additionally, you may also have process keywords like, "Slurry" or "Hard rock". All of these keywords work like metadata to add context to the record as a whole.

Databases that record the keywords associated with data also make the data easier to retrieve and analyze because these keywords become metadata that help identify and label the information for later retrieval.

Artificial Intelligence in library campaigns

Today's automated competitive intelligence can make heavy use of Artificial Intelligence. Artificial Intelligence makes up for some of the deficiencies of the keyword system.

Today, bots use APIs to any of the ChatGPT-style AI engines to gain the following:

- Articles can be summarized.

- Articles can be summarized from a specific viewpoint.

- Emotional values can be assessed to articles to see if they are: positive, negative, or neutral.

- Artificial Intelligence can assign integer values to things that exist on a range, like happiness, perceived value, biases, etc. These integer values and ranges are easily depicted on executive dashboards.

Talent campaigns

Talent campaigns deploy monitoring tactics to watch corporate job postings, or in some cases, LinkedIn profiles. A few talent-related tactics are explored here, but a deeper look at job postings as data sources is described in *Chapter 10, Finding Sources*.

> *A recent phenomenon is that of fake job postings known as "Ghost Postings". They can usually be identified by vague descriptions and jobs that are never filled. They exist for a variety of reasons, including: SEO and shareholder awareness. If you use job postings as a data source, you will need to learn to deal with these.*

Job postings present an easy opportunity to view something from a perspective other than the intended audience. While job seekers see opportunities, real help wanted ads are also lists of organizational needs. An investigator may see these ads for talent as either unsatisfied process inputs, or plans for future investment. These inputs can be monitored for their intelligence value.

Let's assume that we've developed a simple bot that monitors at least one organization's online job postings. Here is some of the analysis that can be done with the collected intelligence.

Time to fill

In addition to recording the existence of individual job postings, it's also important to record when those postings disappear. This should be an indication that the position was filled. If that's the case, the date of disappearance becomes a valuable piece of metadata. If one records a statistically sufficient number of these posting cycles, one can draw conclusions regarding the time it takes to fill such positions, as shown on the facing page.

In the report, we can see an approximation of the number of days it takes Competitor A to fill key software development roles.

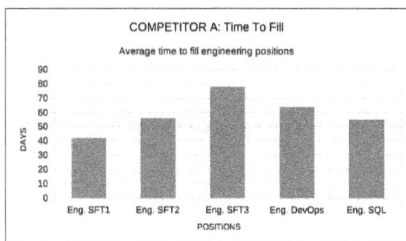

Creating TimeToFill intelligence

If you perform this operation with all of your key competitors, the averaged data becomes an industry standard. This data can be compared and contrasted with your own internal data to measure the efficiency of your own Human Resources department.

If you where to compare those industry averages to your own data, to fill the same roles, you can do some easy self evaluation compare and contrast, as shown below.

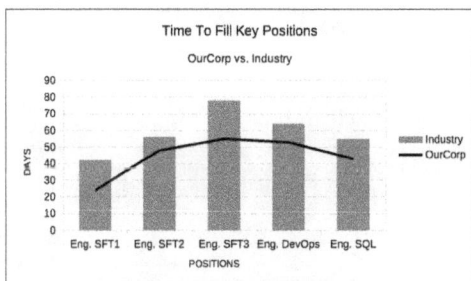

Comparing Time To Fill vs. Industry

If your data looks like OurCorp's in the figure above, then you can be assured of two things.

- You can see that the HR department at OurCorp is exceeding industry standards.

- You have intelligence to figure out how long it will take to hire various types of software developers.

Job postings reflect organizational needs

The previous report charted metadata that was created by recording how long it took to fill jobs. But what other information is being leaked though job postings? Perhaps it's time to look at job postings as a list of corporate needs (or inputs) that can be tracked and trended. It's astonishing how much intelligence is leaked through job postings when you take this perspective.

Predicting competitor's labor needs

If that same bot, used in the last example, also logs unique skills and unique locations, you can find out where or if your competitor is expanding. The bot can be programmed to use locations as keywords, and count where and when those keywords appear in job announcements.

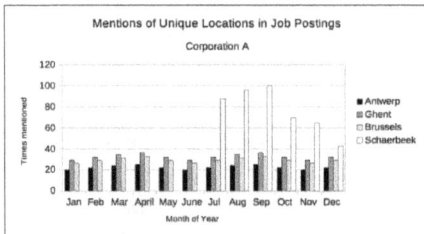

Plotting job locations

A quick look at the data in figure above shows that there isn't much growth (need for resources) in three of the cities where Corporation A operates. But if July through December are any indication, it looks like an expansion into Schaerbeek is definite.

Predicting competitor strategies

Reporting the occurrence of unique keywords is a tactic that can be repeated in various circumstances to achieve various metadata. For example, if we modify that same bot to also harvest unique job positions, we can build a report that shows your competitor's emerging labor needs. This labor is another input that can be used to foresee a competitor's strategic plans.

In the figure below, we repeat the process. In this case, however, we tune the bot to look for unique job positions and to track new skills as they appear. From the data, it's pretty clear that along with the expansion to Schaerbeek, Corporation A is

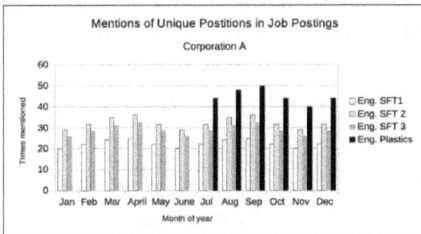

Plotting unique talent requests

also hiring Plastics Engineers, which is new. So, it would appear that they are in the final stages of planning a new plant in Schaerbeek that does something with Plastics Engineering. A closer investigation into the specific job postings would probably tell you exactly what they are doing.

This same technique, of reporting the occurrence of unique phrases can be repeated over and over on varying sets of data to create various intelligence.

Some potential targets for these investigations include, monitoring your competitor's:

- Online advertisements
- Press releases
- Employee directories
- (SEO) Search Engine Optimization habits
- Product lines
- Public filings.

Advantages in recruiting talent

If you haven't noticed, the world is going through a major demographic shift. Global populations are getting older, meaning that a lot of talent is retiring and leaving the job market. Fewer young people are available to replace those professionals. This condition has already hit critical conditions in much of the developed world, including: Germany, China, Korea, and Russia.

We are entering a global talent shortage that is predicted to continue for at least the next twenty years. We know this is true because all of the people, who will be 25-years-old twenty years from now, have already been born and counted. The organizations that can find talent will hold a definite competitive advantage.

The website LinkedIn is fascinating. Not for it's claimed ability to facilitate networking with other professionals, but for the incredible data leak it has become. At one time, employee lists were held as trade secrets. Now they're all published on LinkedIn.

A bot could be developed to first identify every individual on LinkedIn, who works in your industry within the geographic zone of interest to you. That bot could run periodically to keep the list of candidate profiles current.

A second bot could visit that data every week, or so, to look for updates.

Profiles that suddenly switch to "Looking for Opportunities" could be flagged and a notification could immediately be sent to a recruiter. Or better yet, the bot should see this as a call to action and send the individual a message regarding opportunities at your organization.

The number of ways employment advertisements can be used is nearly unlimited. Many of the applications are specific and fill narrow niches. For example a corporate recruiter (head hunter) might employ a competitive intelligence campaign that harvests employee profiles from LinkedIn. This campaign performs analysis to determine, statistically, which of these employed people are most likely to entertain a new opportunity. This list becomes both their new cold call list and a trade secret.

Again, *Chapter 10, Finding sources*, has more to say about job postings as intelligence sources.

Expert interfaces

Sometimes data exists but there are barriers that make it difficult to monitor. Sometimes these difficulties are caused by institutional norms. Other times, sources know that they have valuable intelligence and deliberately make it hard to access to discourage investigators.

Over the years, I have experienced more than one situation where data was available by mandate. And by mandate, I mean that the information was available from a *FOIA*, or *Freedom of Information Act*, request. I've worked with FOIA requests both here in the United States as well as in Europe. In every instance, the data was made available by the *letter of the law*, and not in the *spirit of the law*. A good example of this was the time I was asked to parse, database, and analyze thousands of

FOIA reports from the European Union for a news agency based in The Netherlands. When the EU made the information available, it wasn't in an easily parsable ASCII format. No that would be too easy. The information was delivered in thousands of separate PDF documents that were scanned, usually as skewed and torn images.

As a result, I needed to develop an expert system that converted the scans into text with character recognition software. Then I had to parse away all of the unformatted spaces, tab characters, and line feeds to parse the needed data. As it was, the project was a success and I was told the campaign yielded enough information for three newspaper articles.

The fact that we were able to harvest the data from a hostile source provided the newspaper the competitive advantage of a scoop on the stories. This is the value of expert interfaces. The harder the data is to access, the more valuable the data usually becomes.

The other place I've seen hostile data interfaces is where franchise owners receive market information. I suspect that this information is made available either as a condition of the franchise or because of franchise law. In either case, the data formats remind me of how FOIA requests are commonly done. It's as though people make a deliberate attempt to make the information difficult to access.

I've seen thousand record reports that can only be viewed twenty records at a time. Other interfaces require undocumented experimentation to find where the data is hidden. Fortunately, expert interfaces are a way to tame these unruly websites.

Perhaps the worst example of a hostile interface I've seen was a portal that randomly crashed while downloading reports. Obviously, the first time the website stopped functioning, I assumed there was a problem in my code. After days of debugging, I discovered that the portal stopped functioning after exactly one hundred report requests. As my code took different paths, and downloaded various number of reports at various times, the website would appear to fail unpredictably. This was a difficult problem to resolve. But we probably also had the only automated way of obtaining this extremely valuable market data.

Ad monitoring

Investigators can learn a lot about an organization by monitoring where, and how much, they advertise. Now that the vast majority of advertising is performed online, it makes it easier to compare and contrast advertising strategies of competitors.

Target audience and segmentation

Examining the content, language, and visuals used in competitor's ads can provide insights into their advertising strategy. Understanding how competitors segment their audience can help in refining your own targeting strategy. These choices are reflected in the:

- Types of advertising presented
- Venue selection
- Media type
- The total amount of advertising.

Decades ago, it was more difficult to perform OPSEC on an organization's advertising habits. This was because ad campaigns were conducted on hard-to-monitor media, like: television, radio, newspapers, magazines, printed matchbooks, billboards, direct mail, phone solicitation, or even door-to-door sales.

As of 2023, 61% of all advertising dollars in the United States were spent online[16]. A total of $320 billion was spent on Internet advertising in 2023. That's an 11.3% increase over the year before.

How times have changed.

Much advertising has moved online because that's where people gather. But another force that favors online advertising is that it's easier to audit the performance of an online ad; whereas the ROI on a billboard or television advertisement can be hard to calculate.

Additionally, online ads almost always come with the a call-to-action to purchase the product. You can't do that with a billboard. So these purchases can be tracked in ways that traditional advertising can't. Online advertising is easier to justify because it can not only demonstrate its effectiveness, but in many cases, you are only charged for actual interest in your product (or charged by click).

While the effectiveness of online advertising is attractive, it also opens your organization to leaving a larger OPSEC thumbprint. Every online ad you purchase is a recordable process input that can be tracked and analyzed.

Audits

When one buys traditional advertising it can be difficult to verify that the ads were delivered. With online advertising, however, a bot can monitor where you expect ads to appear to determine if advertisements are actually displayed.

Another interesting piece of intelligence can be found if the website also suggest other products along with your product or ad. This sheds light on where the market positions your

---

[16] Winterberry Group. (2023, May 15). *US online media spend in 2022 and the outlook for 2023 - winterberry group*. - Winterberry Group. https://www.winterberrygroup.com/news/news-posts/us-online-media-spend-in-2022-and-the-outlook-for-2023

products.

Price monitoring

One of the more common competitive intelligence tasks is to monitor competing prices for the same or similar products in the same market. This sounds like a great idea. But before you go down this road be sure you fully describe your objective. In other words, what is your call-to-action? Do you always match (or beat) competing prices?

Project Nessie

Amazon's Project Nessie may have remained cloaked in silence if not referenced multiple times in a complaint filed by the *US Federal Trade Commission*, or US FTC. The FTC complaint doesn't provide the exact purpose of Project Nessie, but it appears that Nessie was set of bots used by Amazon to monitor and control pricing.

The Project Nessie campaign monitored competing websites. Every time Amazon raised a price, Nessie would check if the competing prices were also raised. If Amazon's competitors raised their price to match the new Amazon price, Nessie would maintain the higher price and Amazon would profit from the manufactured inflation. If the competition didn't react to Amazon's price change, they would restore the product to it's original price.

While it sounds insignificant, Amazon allegedly used this campaign to generate profits exceeding $1 billion[17]. In their defense, Amazon claims that the FTC "grossly mischaracterized" what the program did. Amazon also claims to have suspended the program years ago.

---

[17] Amazon made $1 billion through secret price raising algorithm -US FTC | Reuters. (n.d.-b). https://www.reuters.com/legal/new-details-ftc-antitrust-lawsuit-against-amazon-made-public-2023-11-02/

The race to the bottom

Even "value added" retailers want to be priced competitively. The common tactic for being price-competitive is to match the lowest available price. If enough retailers take this approach the entire market becomes depressed. Eventually, prices and margins decrease to the point where no one makes any money. Matching the lowest price isn't competitive, it's suicidal. This is a process I call "*The race to the bottom*".

The obvious way to avoid the race to the bottom is to not compete on price alone. Instead, you can raise the value of the overall experience by providing better customer service, more effective calls-to-action, an easier to use online store, or friction-free return practices.

The other way to avoid the race to the bottom is to not only look for places to lower prices, but to also look for opportunities where you are priced too low and can raise a price without affecting competitiveness.

You might be thinking, "Isn't this what Project Nessie did?" The difference is that Project Nessie manufactured price increases where they didn't already exist. Whereas aligning your price with the market is an adaptation to market fluctuation. Prices comparison creates only a small amount of the intelligence available from online stores.

Retail: compare and contrast

From only two datapoints: price and availability, much metadata can be generated. The following is a non exhaustive list of some examples of this compare and contrast process. The list is probably longer for your specific industry.

Product choices

One of the easiest comparisons to make between competitors is the products they choose to sell. Which products to you have in common and which are exclusive. Why are your product catalogs different? What are those reasons?

Periodic analysis

Earlier you read that websites are often the windows into an organization's internal operations. This is particularly true with online stores. When you periodically monitor entire catalogs of products you start to observe patterns. Then it becomes a game of identifying the cause of these patterns. For example, if a selection of competitors products that all change at the same time, it probably means that they are related in some way. The way the items interrelate is usually industry specific, but that interconnection happens somewhere between procurement and fulfillment.

One way to get a grasp on the source of these group movements is to look at your own inventory. Find cases where groups of your inventory moved in a common way. And then try to identify the cause. You will probably find that these shifts have common causes. Probable causes for inventory group shifts include:

- Supply chain issues
- Recalls
- Seasonal patterns
- Inventory management, close-outs, discontinuations.

Trend analysis

The time at which the collection occurred becomes another piece of metadata. Once time and price are collected for items, that information can be used to characterize past price changes. That characterization can then be manipulated to provide price forecasts and to spot pricing trends.

When those trends appear across your field of competitors, it not only shines light on an industry trend, but it also highlights which of your competitors create trends, and which follow them. When one competitor bucks trends, they are either expressing leadership (watch them) or they are not paying attention to their markets.

Adaptive pricing strategies

The same campaign that detects prices that are out of line with the market should also be capable of correcting that price. At the very least, that software should be able to flag the problem and tell another system to change the price.

Automation can take the delay out of decision making. But before you automate your price changes, you might want to impose some limits to keep things from going awry. For example:

- Limit the price change to a specific percentage of the original price.
- Limit the total number of price updates in a period.
- Limit the total price fluctuation for the period.
- Develop a list of products that do not change.

Updating prices can be a lot of work. If only 1% of prices change in a catalog of 50,000 products you're still updating 500 individual prices. If done by hand, if and each update takes a minute, that's 8.3 hours, or one very long and boring day. Obviously, automation can relieve your staff from mundane and repetitive tasks like price updates. Additionally, computers are faster and more accurate.

Studying competitors' pricing strategies also provides insights into price sensitivity and elasticity within your target market. By observing how changes in prices impact consumer behavior and market dynamics, you can better anticipate how adjustments to your own prices might affect demand, revenue, and profitability.

A more detailed explanation of things that can be observed

from looking at online stores is described in *Chapter 10: Finding sources*, under Surveilling online stores.

TrackRates

One of my personal favorite competitive intelligence projects was a website known as TrackRates.com. TrackRates attempted to solve the problem of how to competitively price hotel rooms.

Hotel rooms are an odd commodity in that the same room can have a lot of value on one day, like the night before The Super Bowl, and very little value the following day. Additionally, a vacant $500 room isn't worth much after midnight. The only way to survive in the hotel industry is to be competitive and you can't be competitive without knowing your market. Without day-by-day pricing and availability information, a hotelier will either be over, or under priced.

TrackRates used multiple bots to track prices on hotel websites. This data was placed in a database where it was organized, analyzed, and made available to hotel managers. This this competitive information, hotel managers could see how their prices compared to their field of competitors. With this information, hotel managers could gauge demand and more competitively price rooms.

Any hotel with competitive pricing intelligence has a distinct competitive advantage. That's the advantage that TrackRates attempted to bring.

With TrackRates, hotel managers could easily see how their rates compared to their marketplace. Just having the ability to tell when a competing hotel was sold-out was a major advantage. Hoteliers could also watch for price and availability trends. In all, TrackRates was a nice example of how competitive intelligence can help hotels identify when to raise prices or when they needed to lower rates to remain competitive.

Further thoughts

While competitive intelligence often involves monitoring your competitors, it does't necessarily mean that you want to copy them. One needs to remember that you won't get ahead by trying to get even.

That's not to say that if you have 20% market share, there isn't something to learn form the company with 40% market share.

While there's emphasis on competitors, that's not all there is to your competitive market. Competitive intelligence includes learning about your supply chain, customers, logistic partners, and sometimes more case-specific requirements like monetary policy, tariffs, weather, infection rates, fish migration patterns, or troop movement.

Any metric that is important to your organization is a potential competitive intelligence input. And those metrics that are specific to your industry often make the most valuable intelligence.

Chapter 6: Monitoring systems

Chapter 7
Tradecraft

Tradecraft is an oddball collection of tools and techniques that don't purely fit the traditional monitoring definition.

Unfortunately people hear the word "tradecraft" the first thing that comes to mind are James Bond spy movies. In competitive intelligence, however, tradecraft is less cinematic. Most of us *in the biz* find little use for exploding pens or submarine cars.

The tradecraft used in competitive intelligence campaigns relies less on exploits and gimmicks and more on mastering the supporting infrastructure to creatively extract, analyze and implement found intelligence.

That's not to say that competitive intelligence tactics shouldn't *borrow* from the basic fundamentals of hacking (anonymity, working remotely, and automation) as described earlier in *Chapter 2, Online intelligence gathering*. But that's where clandestine similarities fade. In contrast, most competitive intelligence campaigns are conducted in brightly lit offices by people who don't manage informants or hold diplomatic passports.

Tradecraft used in competitive intelligence comes and goes as frequently as techniques and trends change. This chapter is in no way exhaustive. But it does describe a few pieces of knowledge and technique that stand out as tradecraft every investigator should know.

Sequential numbers

A lesser known source of intelligence is the metadata left by sequential numbers. The abundance of sequential numbers is astonishing, especially since sequential numbers are both a security threat to those who generate them, and a source of metadata for those who harvest them.

Once you become aware of sequential numbers, you'll notice them everywhere. You'll see them in your car's Vehicle Identification Number, Helpdesk tickets, receipts, checks, and currency. Sequential numbers are everywhere.

Sequential numbers: case study

About a decade ago, I was eager to start an online store. Up to that point, I had experimented with selling a variety of niche items; ranging from shoes for petite women to office supplies. And while I was able to sustain sales, none of these ventures were more than a poorly paying part time job.

One day, I stumbled upon an item that was the ideal online product. Inventory could be sourced from people that wanted to liquidate their holdings. At the same time, I found collectors who were willing to pay top dollar for the same items. The margins were exciting. In one case, inventory was purchased for under a dollar and resold for nearly $110.00. Additionally, the items were easy to store and ship. This was the ideal product to sell online.

A few months in, month-to-month sales were doubling. So profits were plowed back into the business: expanding inventory, erecting shelving, buying shipping supplies, and dedicating space.

After about five months, however, sales unexpectedly slowed to a trickle. Things became so slow that I resorted to buying one of my own items just to ensure that the store still worked.

The online business that started with much promise now felt like a really bad investment. Was my store experiencing a bad month, or was the entire market down? Whatever the case, it looked like I had invested in merchandise that I could no longer sell. More was needed to be known about the dynamics of this market before more investments in inventory were made.

All my merchandise was sold on an eBay style, buy-it-now marketplace that was specific to the industry. There are many similar industry specific marketplaces. Some examples include: Reverb (musical instruments), Airbnb (short-term rentals), Etsy (crafts), Poshmark (used fashion), or Newegg (electronics).

When these niche markets have enough activity, the websites represent demand driven marketplaces. This is important because marketplaces need to be busy enough to have statistical relevance.

While examining the orders, I noticed the order numbers were getting bigger. Being a programmer, and knowing how identifiers (for things like order numbers) are assigned. I looked for, and found, two orders that were placed closely together. To my delight, the order numbers were sequential!

Sequential order numbers were significant because the difference between any two order numbers is the number of orders placed between them, for the entire system. So by subtracting the order numbers from the first order of every month, an idea of how many orders were placed in any month becomes clear.

From the order data available, the total number of orders fulfilled through the system for any month, was equal to the last order number of the month, minus the last order number of the previous month

In the figure below, the numbers in the Order Number column

represent the order of the last order received each month.

In May, for instance, we subtracted April's last order number from the last order number in May to see that approximately 6323 orders had been placed in the system for that month.

Date	Last Order Number	Qty Orders (period)	Change (market size)
April 1	725434	-	-
May 1	731757	6323	-
June 1	738154	6397	101.17%
July 1	744573	6419	100.34%
August 1	750822	6249	97.35%
September 1	757225	6403	102.46%
October 1	763736	6511	101.69%

Market size calculated by order numbers

This process was repeated for all the months where I had data.

After a little analysis, I could see that sales as whole were still strong, and unlike my sales for that month, remarkably stable.

After proving to myself that I hadn't bought into a bubble, and that my small sales slump was nothing more than a statistical anomaly, I set off to find more uses for these sequential order numbers.

I determined that our mean sale (the average, minus a few outliers) was $19.43. From that, I could calculate plausible sales for the entire sales channel.

From the meager sales data I collected, I was able to extrapolate the sales volume of the entire channel, as shown below.

Month	Qty Orders (period)	Sales, (entire channel)
May	6323	$122,855.89
June	6397	$124,293.71
July	6419	$124,721.17
August	6249	$121,418.07
September	6403	$124,410.29
October	6511	$126,508.73

Estimating the total sales for the entire channel

This information made me wonder how much money the owners of the website were making. The owners of the channel made a 20% commission on every sale, plus $1.25 of the shipping charge they assessed the buyers. So if the typical sale was $19.43, that meant they made ($19.43*0.2) + $1.25, or $5.13, per sale.

As seen from the data in the figure below, this simple website was generating a cool $380,000 a year from commissions and shipping charges.

Date	Qty Orders (period)	Sales, (entire channel)	Channel Profit
May	6323	$122,855.89	$32,436.99
June	6397	$124,293.71	$32,816.61
July	6419	$124,721.17	$32,929.47
August	6249	$121,418.07	$32,057.37
September	6403	$124,410.29	$32,847.39
October	6511	$126,508.73	$33,401.43

Estimating the total profit for the entire channel

Since the website was never updated and never advertised it could have been operated by one person in a few hours a month. This was a pretty nice side hustle for someone. Their business model was clearly better than mine!

Sequential numbers as intelligence

Competitive intelligence investigators gain opportunities when sequential numbers are used as unique identifiers.

- Sequential numbers, when used as unique identifiers, inadvertently count the number of times something happened. That could be the number of orders placed (in the case of order numbers) or the number of vehicles made (in the case of serial numbers).

- Sequential numbers accidentally time-order the sequence in which things happened. For example, if you have three order numbers from the same source, you probably know the sequence the orders were placed based on their order numbers.

- Sequential numbers provide particularly strong intelligence when they are paired with a date. Sometimes this happens when an identifier, like an order number, is directly associated with a date, as on a receipt. Once the relationship between a sequential number and a date are established, you can determine how many of those things occurred between two dates. With this tactic, you can create metadata to create evidence of many things.

  For example,

    - If order numbers are sequential and tied to a date, you can determine how many orders were placed between any two dates.

    - If product identifiers are both sequential and associated with a date, you can describe the sequence that new products were added to the catalog, when they were added, and the period between new additions.

- If individual items have serial numbers, and a date is associated with that number, you can tell how many of those things were made within a specific period. If you have a history of this data, you can project how many will be made in the future based on historic trends.

More sequential numbers in the real world

As mentioned earlier, once one becomes aware of sequential numbers, they appear everywhere, including in the physical world. A few years ago, I presented a talk on metadata[18] where I profiled the gross sales of a fast food restaurant by analyzing order numbers. I began this campaign by making a small purchase in the store. Then I drove through the drive-up window to purchase a drink. I quickly compared the two receipts and verified that the orders had sequential numbers. Additionally, I verified that both the front register and the drive-up register worked from the same system, and generated order numbers the same way.

I made a small purchase every day at the same time for about two weeks. By using the (sequential) order numbers, I was able to capture the store's day-to-day sales by subtracting one day's order number from the next. Even in that short amount of time, weekly patterns were starting to emerge.

My last purchase was made with the intent of eating inside while I wrapped-up the campaign. One last thing I wanted to know was the average order value. With this information, I could estimate sales values, and not just the number of orders filled. As I worked and ate my meal, it was easy to hear the cashier announce the value of each order. I collected this information until I had something that I felt was statistically

---

[18] Strata Data Conference San Jose 2018, Speaker: Michael Schrenk "Understanding Metadata", San Jose, CA, USA March 5, 2018

significant. With this metadata, I was able to approximate total daily sales for that store.

The German tank problem

Allied Forces heard rumors that Germany was building more tanks than expected. If true, this would have an great impact on the D-Day Invasion as each fully operational tank also required a support staff of roughly 90 troops. And for every tank, there were another nine trucks and two half-tracks, carrying: troops, fuel, ammunition, food and water.

Up to this point, tank quantities were estimated though spies making visual observations. Spying, however, is expensive, dangerous, and slow. Furthermore, no one knew how accurate that intelligence was.

The Allies had a small number of captured and destroyed tanks in their possession. From captured or destroyed tanks they noticed that the Germans had attached sequential serial numbers to gearboxes. With this limited information, and some experimentation, they developed the following formula, which proved successful.[19]

$$QtyTanks^{Est} = Serial^{max} + \frac{Serial^{max} - Observations^{Qty}}{Observations^{Qty}}$$

Where:

$QtyTanks^{Est}$	is the estimated number of tanks
$Serial^{max}$	is the highest serial number discovered
$Observations^{Qty}$	is the total number of serial numbers collected

Solution to the German Tank Problem

---

[19] Ruggles, R., & Brodie, H. (1947). An empirical approach to economic intelligence in World War II. Journal of the American Statistical Association, 42(237), 72–91. https://doi.org/10.1080/01621459.1947.10501915

The formula is easy to understand once you realize what it's doing. Imagine each observed serial number placed on a number line. The assumption is that, all things being equal, the space between 0 and the first serial number should be the same as the last serial number and the final answer. The formula essentially calculates the average space between serial numbers and adds that value to the highest serial number.

After the war, it was verified that this formula very closely estimated the actual number of tanks produced.

Date	Estimate (Spies)	Estimate (Statistical)	German Records
Jun 1940	1000	169	122
Jun 1941	1550	244	271
Aug 1942	1550	327	342

Calculated tank estimates were more accurate than observed estimates.

While it's often important to serialize items, it is seldom advantageous to assign sequential numbers. A much better approach is to assign random numbers, that perhaps correspond to actual numbers. Or to assign letter values to digits, as shown below, and change the code periodically.

B	L	A	C	K	S	T	O	N	E
0	1	2	3	4	5	6	7	8	9

A number to letter obfuscation technique

The German Tank Problem is a well known statistical exploit. And has been used to solve other problems in medicine and sociology. There was also a famous attempt to estimate the total number of Commodore 64 computers built.[20] So it is surprising

---

[20] Barnes, R. (2017, March 16). *Sales soar and Raspberry Pi beats Commodore 64*. Raspberry Pi Official Magazine. https://magazine.raspberrypi.com/articles/raspberry-pi-sales

that this technique was also useful during the Korean War and by US Generals, who got a private tour of an Israeli tank factory.

Creating local monopolies

In the beginning of this chapter, you learned how competitive intelligence was used to validate that a drop in sales was a fluke, and not caused by getting into a market too late. But as often happens, solving one problem reveals another. Though sales were back, sourcing a steady supply of inventory for eager buyers was becoming a problem.

Fortunately, with a little competitive intelligence, the marketplace where I sold could also solve my procurement problem. I soon learned that I could develop a bot that scanned for situations that could be exploited.

For example, the table below depicts an active market where I and two other sellers each have an identical product for sale, for prices ranging from $12.79 to $15.99.

Seller	Price	Qty Available
Me	$12.79	1
Seller 1	$14.78	1
Seller 2	$15.99	1
Average	$14.52	-
Total	$43.56	3

A competitive market for a unique product

This data shows opportunities for at least two potential actions. The first, and most obvious call-to-action is that there is nearly two dollars separating our product from the next most competitive offering. If nothing else, there is an opportunity to raise a price without seriously affecting competitiveness.

The second opportunity is buying the remaining inventory from the other two sellers. Once purchased, we could have a situation as depicted the next table.

Seller	Price	Qty Available
Me	$19.95	1
Me	$21.95	1
Me	$23.95	1
Average	$21.95	
Total	$65.85	3

Post monopoly realities

For an investment of around $30.00, I was able to procure inventory that I can resell for $46.00. Plus, now that I have a local monopoly for this item, I can also raise the price of my original item by $7.00. Once all three items sell, the total impact of this $30 purchase is $53.00. There's little downside to this campaign. It provides a demonstrable competitive advantage in a market where sales are easy, but little inventory is available on the wholesale market.

Such campaigns point out the importance of automation. It would be prohibitively expensive to hire someone to search through the thousands of products to find situations where the math works to our advantage. With automation, however, it's fairly straight forward to write a bot that looks for high volume products with few sellers, with price spreads large enough to engage.

This particular campaign is also a good example of why anonymity and remote execution are important. If the owner's of the website knew that I was conducting this campaign, they may want to shut me down. So it is imperative that this trade secret remain a secret. This meant that I could not be overtly obvious about my activities. So the bot was written to mimic human behaviors and not produce an undue amount of traffic.

I long suspected that other bots were running on this platform because competing prices where often lowered to exactly $0.01 below mine shortly after my prices were adjusted. Since it was a seller's market, I never did develop a price matching bot. Instead, I spent most of my time on procurement campaigns.

Websites are windows into organizations

As seen in the sequential number examples, artifacts left on websites can become clues into the internal operation of the organization that runs the website. Another prime example of where this occurs is in query strings, or the string of text that exists after a "?" symbol in a URL, as shown below.

```
https://www.someMarketPlace.com?
customerId=1943&report=listOrders&rows=20
```

A query string with artifacts

The URL in the figure above could be intended to request an order history for a customer identified by customerID. Query strings, like the one above, appear in both links and as a result of form submissions. You might also see similar query strings in embedded in the JavaScript found on webpages.

These artifacts are important because they are literal windows into how backend systems work. You can obtain valuable intelligence if you know enough about a target's backend servers. Focus on everything that appears after the "?" in a query string. These name/value pairs are the names and values for system variables that are used by the code that runs on the server. The variables in the example shown include; a customerID, a report type, and the number of rows to include in the report.

If this customerID is typical, we can assume that customerID is an auto incremented index into the database's customer table.

As such, the customer, whose ID is 1942, was the customer who signed-up just before me. It also indicates that there were 1942 customers at the time I became a customer. *Theoretically,* if we applied the full URL with a sellerID different than our own, we could expect to see their sales report.

The fact that there's a variable called "report" is an indication that there are reports other than a list of orders. This is interesting information, as it may pique our observation skills into finding more reports. But I'd be hesitant to venture further out of fears of leaving strange records in log files and subsequently being discovered.

While I have reservations in experimenting with the "report" variable, I'd have no qualms manipulating the "row" variable.

Often, websites will make reports available but the data isn't always conveniently accessible. For example, a website might force a user to download a 2000 line report in 20 row increments, as is the default for this website.

There is no way I'd write a bot that downloaded a report a hundred times if I had the opportunity to request the entire report at once. In my opinion, this is a stealthier method than making those requests individually.

Unintended leaks

Sometimes unintentional leaks appear as artifacts of marketing activity. These leaks happen from time to time, and are never planned. Perhaps the real value of these leaks is to sharpen the eye of the investigator. One of my favorite marketing leaks was something called *Amazon Purchase Circles*[21].

It's difficult to determine the origin of Purchase Circles, but one can assume that someone at Amazon thought it would be

---

[21] Writer, C. S., CBR Staff Writer CBR Online legacy content, Writer, C. S., & content, C. O. legacy. (1999, August 29). *Amazon modifies controversial " purchase circles" feature.* https://techmonitor.ai/technology/ amazon_modifies_controversial_purchase_circles_feature

interesting for readers to see what books are popular in their area[22]. They did this by grouping purchases made within specific IP addresses.

Identifying geographic locations by IP address is sketchy at best. This method doesn't identify the location of users as much as it identifies where their private network accesses the Internet. But the real failing of Amazon Purchase Circles is that it provided too much unintentional information.

Amazon deliberately limited Purchase Circles to IP addresses with 200 readers to protect individual privacy. The result was Purchase Circles from places like Boulder City Nevada. The problem is that large corporate campuses, like Apple, looked like small communities of readers. I distinctly remember using Purchase Circles to see what Apple employees were buying from their corporate campus. Many of their purchases were obviously personal, and probably bought over employee lunch periods. But other, more technical purchases, exposed an intense interest in optical recognition.

Google search operators

While it's not automated, manual search engine queries can be a very valuable part of a competitive intelligence campaign, especially in the early or planning stages.

While most people merely type what they want to find into a search, most search engines, particularly Google, will provide very specific search capability. Sometimes these specific searches provide surprising results.

---

[22] Press Center. (1999, August 20). *Amazon.com introduces "purchase circles(tm)" featuring thousands of bestseller lists for hometowns, workplaces, universities, and more*. Press Center. https://press.aboutamazon.com/1999/8/amazon-com-introduces-purchase-circlestm-featuring-thousands-of-bestseller-lists-for-hometowns-workplaces-universities-and-more

Google Hacking (Google dorking)

The profession closest to competitive intelligence is probably Investigative Journalism. On several occasions, I've presented mini "hacking workshops" to help European Journalists get more from their online research. *Google Hacking*, or expertly using search queries was always a large part of those workshops. In some circles this practice is also known as *Google Dorking*.

As an instructor, it was fascinating to see what happened when tools were placed in the hands of truly creative people. After only minutes of practice, these journalists were creating Google queries that found all sorts of things that they shouldn't have found. These treasures ranged from: lists of passwords, private financial statements, to video feeds from security cameras.

Search basics

While these are called "Google" search operators, you'll find that they have become fairly standardized and should work in a variety of search environments, including Bing.com, DuckDuckGo.com, and most others.

The figure below shows three basic searches.

```
#1      "Chocolate Chip Cookies"
#2      "Bank -River"
#3      "Cats | Dogs"
```

Simple search operators

Search terms, placed in quotes, represent an exact match. For example, the first example above requests links to webpages that directly contain the string "Chocolate Chip Cookies". This query should provide some assurance that the search results for webpages about other types of cookies will not be returned.

The second example requests links to webpages that contain the word "Bank" that don't also contain the word "River". The intent here is for search results that return references to financial institutions only.

In the third example, links to webpages that contain either the word "Cat" or "Dog" will be returned.

The *site operator*, as shown in the next figure, limits the search results to those that were found on a specific website.

```
#1      site:mepso.com "Spying on Success"
#2      Site:ebay.com Contact
```

Limiting searches to a single website

In the search criteria above, the first example should provide links to this book's webpage on the publisher's website. The second example is something you'd type to find the list of contacts at eBay.

I have found that these searches, conducted through a search engine, are much more productive than one-site searches allowed on many website. The difference is that the Google search doesn't have internal filters that limit results.

Searching for files

Search operators allow you to search for more than webpages. You can use search engines to find any kind of file. As long as there is a link to these files, they will eventually show up on webpages.

The figure below shows a few possibilities for finding documents that aren't webpages.

```
#1      filetype:pdf
#2      filetype:xls
#3      filetype:doc "competitive intelligence"
#4      filetype:xls "sales" site:competitor.com
```

Searching for files other than webpages.

Searching within page titles

One of the more interesting search operators is the *intitle: operator*. The intent of this search operator is to make it easier to find relevant pages. For example, the first search term in the next figure would be a traditional use of this operator, to find a webpage about

```
#1      intitle: "Chihuahuas"
#2      intitle:"index of"
#3      Intitle:"contact"
#4      intitle:"index of"
#5      intitle:"index of /bank/" site:FederalBankofIgsoliva.com
```

intitle hacking

While the intitle operator was intended to locate subjects significant enough to appear in a webpages title, it quickly caught the eye of hackers and was put to other use. What wasn't originally considered was that often, error codes, maintenance flags, and default messages are left in titles as well. As such, this operator makes it very easy to find sloppy coding and applications installed with (known) default settings intact.

Index of /php

Name	Last modified	Size	Description
Parent Directory		-	
notes/	2024-05-06 08:14	-	
backup/	2024-05-06 08:14	-	
contact_me.php	2019-03-12 13:36	1.1K	

Discovering unprotected directories

For example, the search term 'intitle: "index of"' will provide links to pages that show the entire contents (every file and directory) of a directory on the web server. Furthermore, you can click on the files to download them, and click on the directories to drill deeper into the directory structure.

A hacker might search for "intitle:index of php" to find situations like the one below, where entire directories are publicly accessible can be surfed by anyone who knows they're there.

Some other things to think about when searching on title contents include:

- System error conditions are often included in the titles of webpages. Searching on known errors can reveal servers that are open to potential exploit.

- The "intitle:" operator can be used to find default phrases that are used on many *Internet of Things,* or *Internet peripherals,* like security cameras, baby monitors, doorbell cameras, etc.

Carefully crafted queries find Internet-aware peripherals in specific regions. Techniques like this have been used in the Russian/Ukrainian war to monitor doorbell cams to track Russian troops in occupied territories[23].

You're be surprised what you can find when you conduct a focused search on credentials and usernames. Even a simple search like: `filetype:csv "passwords"`, is apt to provide an eye-opening list of victims.

The list of Google search operator continues to evolve. One operator that is on its way out is the *cache:* operator. The cache: operator allows one to view the previously stored version of a webpage. This information is needed so the search engine can detect changes, among other things. Perhaps it's most common, and useful, application is to circumvent paywalls. An example

---

[23] https://www.hackers-arise.com/post/we-have-successfully-accessed-many-ip-cameras-in-ukrainian-territory-to-spy-on-russian-activities

of this use is shown in the next Figure.

```
cache: https://www/YourPaywalledWebSite.com
```

Defeating paywalls with cache:

Google claims that they are deprecating this operator. But, it still works as of the writing of this book.

Secrets in plain sight (Franken v. Coleman)

Sometimes very private data is left in public places. An excellent example is what happened in the 2006 Minnesota Senatorial election, primarily between Norm Coleman, and former Saturday Night Live writer and talk show host, Al Franken.

The two candidates were polar opposites, Coleman representing the traditional Republican values, while the Democrat, Franken advocated for progressive policies such as universal healthcare and environmental protection.

The campaign was highly negative. Coleman accused Franken of being an out-of-touch Hollywood liberal, while Franken criticized Coleman for his close ties to big business and special interests. In the end, Coleman was declared the winner by 215 votes. However, after several mandated recounts and court challenges, Franken won by 225 votes[24]. As interesting as that story was, there's a more interesting story involving a data leak.

The donor "leak"

As the story goes, an IT person for the Coleman campaign left a spreadsheet of donor information, unprotected, on the campaign's server. This data was very explosive as it included donor names, addresses, dates, contributions, and even credit

---

[24] Democrat wins Minnesota Senate seat in recount | reuters. (n.d.). https://
       www.reuters.com/article/us-usa-politics-minnesota/democrat-wins-
       minnesota-senate-seat-in-recount-idUSTRE50405S20090105

card numbers. The leaked data became widely available on many of the Internet's hacker channels. Once the mainstream news stories were published, allegations of hacking followed shortly. We later learned that the actual cause of the data leak, like many, was carelessness.

The public web server was probably a very convenient place to keep a list of donors, but from a security standpoint, it is a dangerous practice. This file was left on the \db\ directory in publicly accessible webspace. So, it wasn't hard to find.

Perhaps someone at Democratic Headquarters got curious on Google one day and performed a Google search similar to the one below:

```
"Coleman" filetype:csv
```

Or, maybe it looked more like this one.

```
"Coleman" "donor" filetype:csv
```

In either case, if you type the text from above into a Google search box it will return many links to CSV files that are in some way related to the subject. The returned links are mostly election results and candidate lists, but I suspect someone did a slightly more refined search and found the donor file mentioned earlier, which was probably (sloppily) linked by a misinformed staffer.

Spreadsheets, video feeds, raw file directories, and other untraditional media, all appear in search results. The search engine just needs to find it. This is aided by the fact that people have bad habits. Some of these habits include: leaving files and directories unprotected, or not properly configuring Internet appliances and servers, or leaving them in default conditions.

Guessing where things will be

A large software company had the tradition of publishing their annual report on their website. Important information is often disclosed in these reports, so the people with first access to this information become the first-to-know how to manage their shares of stock. One creative investigator discovered that the year of publication was the only part of the URL for the published report that changed from year-to-year. They also discovered that the report was available, at the predicted date, days before the official publication date.

Snipers

It always amazes me what years of industry-specific knowledge and a bit of curiosity can accomplish. Over they years, I've had the opportunity to work with very creative clients on some pretty amazing competitive intelligence projects. As much as I enjoyed these projects, I can't talk or write about most of these campaigns because they remain trade secrets. But, there is one exception where enough time has passed that one client has kindly given permission to share this one project. That was the project where a campaign bought millions of dollars of cars over a period of about nine months[25].

A retail automotive client was experiencing difficulty in acquiring quality used cars for resale. A traditionally reliable source for such cars are rental car agencies, as they generally don't rent the same car longer than two years. Once out of service, they need a way to dispose of these late model, low mileage, cars. Some rental car companies sell retired rental cars directly to consumers. But most rental companies prefer to scale operations and auction their retired cars directly to dealers, like my client.

My client grew frustrated with the website that ran these auctions. There were cars that could easily fill holes in his inventory, but he was never able to buy them. The problem was largely caused by a very poorly designed website.

---

[25] " How my Botnet purchased millions of dollars in cars and defeated the Russian hackers", DEF CON 21, August 2013. https://www.youtube.com/watch?v=sgz5dutPF8M

Cars and descriptions of cars, available for sale that day, appeared on the auction website early in the morning. But you could not purchase one of the cars until noon. It was at that moment when a "Buy Now" button would appear next to individual cars, but only if you refreshed the webpage after twelve pm.

This sales method had the disadvantage of putting a lot of stress on the server. As such, the auction website's server dragged to a crawl everyday at noon, because everyone was busy refreshing their browser. Additionally, of the approximately 350 cars available every morning, there would maybe be five cars that 80% of the dealerships in the country wanted. So there was also high competition for individual vehicles.

The architecture of the auction website led to odd usage. For example, in car dealership lunchrooms around the country, every available sales person, parts manager, and administrative assistant would be positioned around a table. In front of them, laptop computers with the auction website on their screen. They'd each be responsible for a different car, or the same car if they really wanted it. As midday drew nearer, they'd press the browser refresh button as quickly as they could, until a "Buy Now" button appeared. When the buy button appeared (at noon), they'd attempt to buy the car. But in many to most cases, the website would just time-out.

What was required here was an expert interface that solved these access problems. My client called one morning in desperation. There were dealerships getting deals, but they weren't his! He explained the situation and asked for help. Here's what we came up with.

We developed a private website, where he could view all the cars that would be available for sale at noon. These cars were found by bots that scraped the website for this information earlier in the day. So now, instead of assembling a team to frantically hit refresh buttons during their lunch break, he could relax and select cars while drinking his morning coffee.

He could select up to five cars and then forget about it until noon. At noon the bot attempted to purchase the selected vehicles. If the purchase attempt was successful, the bot would arrange for payment and delivery. The client would shortly thereafter receive a report telling him how many he bought.

As the bots grew closer to the auction time, they started to synchronize clocks to the auction site's time/date server. This was done to measure the delays in a busy network. Done repeatedly, this gave the bots enough information to predict how long *before* the auction they needed to submit their request so it could compete with all the other network traffic and *still* arrive at the destination at exactly 12:00.

We apparently got pretty good at this because we soon were scoring around ninety-five percent of the cars requested. This was up form zero percent; my client was ecstatic!

We worked this system for the best part of the year. And then suddenly our success rates started to drop precipitously. It appeared we had competition. My client researched the source of our troubles, as only he could, and discovered a group working in another region. They apparently also had software.

It was clear that the current process wasn't working any more. So we abandoned the chronographic approach. Instead, for every car that my client desired, software would fire-off sixteen bots, each delayed a sub second from the next. One of those bots was apt to get lucky to time it correctly and purchase the car. Most of the bots failed, but enough got through for the client to once again, get nearly every car he wanted.

As with all good things, this campaign didn't last forever. But by the time the program was over, the bots had purchased millions of dollars of easy-to-sell inventory.

What I learned from this project was the importance of building

ROI, or Return on Investment tools directly into the project, because this tactical competitive intelligence campaign was very profitable.

Creating scarcity

Only after market awareness is achieved can you begin to identify unique products that are not currently available in your market. This is important information because when you introduce a unique product, you have control over the supply, which also means you control the price. In other words, you have more pricing freedom when you own the market for a particular product.

Let's say that your city has three scooter dealerships. And that you are responsible for managing inventory for one of those stores.

You commissioned a bot that provides a daily update of your competitor's inventories from their websites. This data is very useful because not only does it indicate how your competitor's price their inventory, it also provides insight on what they choose to stock. By comparing daily reports, you can see which scooters are no longer available for sale and assumed sold. That provides an opportunity to create metadata that indicates how long it takes to sell specific scooters and which scooters have most demand.

Since all three scooter stores are located in the same city, they share a common market. You assume customers in this market research before they purchase. So what your competitors stock, how inventory is selected, and how items are price should reflect customer preferences.

Software can look at the inventory data to provide evidence of quick moving inventory, scooters that aren't selling well, and products that are over or under stocked. All of this information should make you, as inventory manager, more effective.

You essentially game the supply and demand curves when you create scarcity by stocking variations of inventory items that your competition doesn't stock. These unique products may actually increase the size of your market by pulling customers from neighboring markets. People will travel a distance when they know you have something unique, discoverable, desirable, and scarce.

Here's another way of looking at this tactic. Assume that, in total, the three scooter dealerships in this market have a total of twenty-three 50cc scooters for sale, all of them blue. Knowing this, you jump at an opportunity to acquire an *orange* 50cc scooter.

Realtime awareness of your market made it easy to spot an opportunity, knowing that this unique scooter will sell quickly, and for a premium price, simply because it wasn't blue. When the orange scooter was procured for inventory, it expanded the market for orange scooters, because there wasn't one before. And, it simultaneously created a scarcity for orange 50cc scooters because there was only one. Without the existence of an orange scooter in the market, the customer would have probably purchased a blue one, at the going price, and without real urgency. But when you have market awareness, these procurement decisions become easier.

Generally speaking, there is a market price for everything. The final sale price may deviate by a few percentage points, but if two retailers are selling the same product in the same market, they will have very similar prices. That's because these prices are determined by supply and demand and are quite predictable. The fact that retail prices are "fixed" by market demands means that smart retailers make their money not by selling at market prices, but by sourcing their products more competitively. Successful retailers know that it's easier to procure inventory smartly than it is to manipulate a mature retail market.

Merging unaligned markets

As the last example showed, it's much easier to compare and contrast markets when you have software to gather and analyze prices and availability for you.

There are opportunities when local markets don't operate under the same supply and demand curves of global markets. When markets are out of alignment, it opens opportunities to buy on the lower priced market and resell on the market with higher prices.

There are many examples of these market imbalances and all of them create opportunities. Perhaps one of the best examples are the queues of busses carrying US senior citizens across either the Mexican or Canadian boarders to have their prescriptions filled. Another example are the Viagra equivalents sold by pharmacies in East Asia. This market is so unbalanced that the same chemical compound is sold for over $80.00 a tablet in the United States or less than $0.20, after importing it from India.

What causes these massive differences in prices? The most probable culprits are differing:

- Supply and costs
- Local demand
- Government subsidies
- Greed.

Pricing is often driven by scarcity, whether real or created. The fact that Pfizer is the only supplier of Viagra in the United States means that they can set their price anywhere they like. This is how much of the healthcare prices are set in the United States. And when a customer's choices are dying or not dying, it blows-away the supply and demand theories because people will pay anything to continue living.

Another prime example of unbalanced markets is the practice procuring textbooks from publishers in developing economies and reselling those texts in developed markets. This practice creates two benefits: it facilitates the foreign publisher to further leverage their investments, and it brings modern textbooks to places where they are needed.

In these arrangements, the publisher generally sells the publishing rights to a foreign publisher, who produces the book locally. Sometimes the locally produced books are printed on lower quality paper with smaller fonts and smaller pages. But the books are essentially the same.

Before the Internet, it was difficult to detect that these market differences existed. But today, with bots, finding opportunities is only limited by ones imagination. In the case of textbooks, a cottage industry exists on many college campuses, where highly discounted "international editions" of textbooks are sold to incoming freshmen. This cottage industry exists because the new students are able to purchase new books for a fraction of what used books cost in the bookstore.

Some argue that realigning markets is a legitimate business practice that capitalizes on market inefficiencies, while others view it as ethically questionable, especially if it involves exploiting governmental subsidies in developing nations. In some cases, as in the case of healthcare, it's obvious that there are excessive profits made at the expense of people's welfare.

Social media tradecraft

Sometimes you can get lucky and find a function in social media that fulfills a competitive intelligence objective. I once needed to find images of email account holders. I found the easiest way to do this was to perform a Facebook search with the email addresses. In probably 80% of the searches, a profile image was found to correlate with the email address. This was a very useful campaign.

There have been several occasions where I have used

competitive intelligence to help law enforcement and private investigators solve cases. In one such case, I worked with a *Private Investigator*, who was on the trail of someone pretending to be the wife of a well-known athlete on social media.

This was more than a *fan account*, as the poster leaked a daily stream of personal information including where she was and who she was with. Perhaps the most troubling aspect were the original (not copied) photographs of the client that were posted regularly. So whoever this was, they had close physical contact with the client.

The situation freaked me out. Even though I do similar things professionally, my targets are always organizations and governments. I believe that citizens have a responsibility to monitor powerful groups that influence politics and economies. But in this case, there was an individual mimicking another while leaking massive amounts of personal information. Perhaps the most troubling thing is that this person's motives were unknown.

We were able to "discover" the impostor with a little tradecraft. The trick I used was to post *special images* on her wall. The images were special because as they are loaded from the server, they also execute a program. I call these exploits *executable images* and have talked about them in the past at DEF CON[26]. In this case, I developed a small piece of code that exchanged a cookie with the viewer's browser when they viewed the image. The image was strategically placed on both the impostor's and the victim's walls. Every time either account was viewed the extra software in the image collected IP addresses, counters, the query string, and other information. The query string was particularly important because there was a bug that exposed the screen name of the person viewing the page. The IP address

---

[26]   *DEF CON 15 - Michael Schrenk - The Executable Image Exploit.*
https://www.youtube.com/watch?v=RW0-qBeopcA

also proved valuable in geolocating the impostor. After a few days of collection, the Private Investigator was able to triangulate enough intelligence to identify the impostor.

Further thoughts

If you want to learn more tradecraft scan some of the available hacking books. Or better yet, attend a hacking conference like DEF CON[27]. One thing is certain, you will learn more about tradecraft form the people that create it than you will form people that develop products to protect against it.

The other certainty is that tradecraft comes and goes. What worked in one campaign may not work in the next. Part of this is because exploits get blocked. Other times, old technology is replaced with better technology.

The other thing to remember about tradecraft is that it is often extremely task specific. For example, there were techniques used in the sniper example that will never be available again because the process used by the industry has changed.

---

[27]   www.defcon.org

Spying on Success

Chapter 8
Tactics and ethics

As we saw earlier with the *Dirty Tricks Scandal*, ethics are a tool to keep exuberant tactics from running out of hand.

Many people mistake ethics for *doing the right thing*. But the actual definition of Ethics are what you do when you are forced to make one choice between two bad options. At least that is the classical definition of the word. Modern speakers have informally enlarged the definition of the word "ethics" to include decisions that deserve an obvious good and evil response. So, the modern day definition of ethics also includes morals or *moral discernment*.

The primary rule

Defined ethics are important in competitive intelligence because ethics guide the campaign through difficult choices. Fortunately, competitive intelligence ethics are simple and boil down to,

> *Touch your sources as little as possible.*

You don't want to access information on a server any more than absolutely needed. Any other approach may bring unwanted attention to your campaign and result in it's discovery and eventual take down. So in this case, ethics is a survival skill.

I learned this lesson fairly early in my competitive intelligence career. At the time, I was working on a campaign that required large numbers of court records. It was a Friday and I had a goal to produce data by the following Monday. I decided to develop a bot to collect the needed data over the weekend.

That was my first mistake. It is highly recommended that you conduct campaigns like this during regular business hours, and not at night or over weekends. The reason is that your traffic will be mixed with everyday traffic. If you operate outside that schedule, the records you place in the source server's log file will stand alone and be more obvious.

Once I started the bot I quickly realized that it was not going to meet the goal of collecting the required data by Monday. The bot was throttled to run slowly because, even at that time, I knew that running bots slowly, with random delays, was key to making bots look human and less discoverable.

The need for data led to an ethical lapse. It was a weekend, I thought, who cared if I ran my bot faster than normal? Further, I reasoned that since it was Saturday, I wasn't interfering with their regular business.

I rewrote the bot to run as quickly as it could and started it up again. This time the bot ran as fast as the court's server would allow. After seeing that it was running correctly, I left it to run on it's own while I did something else.

A short time later, I returned and saw the bot had crashed. I immediately looked to see the last page it downloaded to get an indication of what the problem was.

The problem was that instead of the page of court data the bot was expecting, it was confronted with a message from the court system telling me that I was in violation of their Terms of Agreement, that I faced felony charges, and that I should call the number on the page first thing Monday morning.

It was obvious what I should have done. But now, instead of disappointing a client because of data delays, I had to face the wrath of a state court system.

The following Monday, I called the number and was straightforward in who I was and what I was doing. The overworked IT person on the other end suggested I run my bots slower in the future. I got off the phone without so much as a hand slap. But that lesson has remained with me all these years.

Conversion

Conversion is the legal term for doing something that prevents another person from enjoying the use of their property. Some examples of conversion include:

- Erecting a billboard that blocks another billboard
- Borrowing an automobile without the owner's permission
- Failing to return borrowed property
- Blocking an easement.

With conversion, the ownership doesn't change, but control does. Conversion doesn't only apply to real property; it also applies to data and servers.

Trespass to servers

There are many examples of developers that requested so much data from their sources that they made the source unusable for everyone else. Perhaps the most famous story is that of a website named Bidders Edge. Bidders Edge was an auction aggregator back in the day when eBay had competitors. Bidders Edge wanted to be an aggregated search of all auction sites. To do this, they had to scrape each and every auction page from each source repeatedly through the day. At one point they produced so much traffic that eBay had to increase their server capacity, just to maintain their own traffic, and that of the aggregator. Eventually eBay sued Bidders Edge in a landmark case that established that the law of trespass also extends to the Internet.

Trespass to booking systems

One of the more interesting cases of trespass was the case of an unnamed Asian Airline[28] that found a creative way to monopolize markets and raise prices.

In 2017, software developers for an Southeast Asian airline found a particular feature in their competitor's reservation system. This feature was actually a process step that allowed passengers to reserve a ticket, and then finalize their travel plans (seat selection, baggage needs, etc.) before paying for their airline ticket. When a user added a ticket to their online shopping cart within the reservation system, the airline would temporarily hold that ticket for fifteen minutes. During this window, the ticket remained unavailable to other customers. Only if the fifteen-minute period elapsed without the ticket being purchased, would the seat become available again.

The airline developed a competitive intelligence campaign to make incomplete reservations on competing routes. The campaign essentially made competing seats unavailable; giving the airline the only available seats on many routes, forcing travelers to book flights on the airline running the campaign. Since they had temporary monopolies on these routes, the fares increased appropriately.

The practice was discovered when several airlines noticed a sudden increase in the number of incomplete bookings on their websites. These antics were easily traced back to the airline in question.

---

[28] Believe me, I have tried to identify the airline, but for now this story will be shrouded in online mystery. I suspect the airline would do better without the publicity. From the best I can guess, the airline was somewhere in Southeast Asia.

Click fraud

Another example of interference is click fraud[29]. Click fraud occurs when a person, or bot, clicks on an advertisement or link with the intent of misrepresenting an actual web surfer. This practice is used to create fake interactions with advertisements which cost advertisers money. Other times, click fraud is used to make websites look like they are more popular than they are.

While illegal, click fraud is rampant. There are services where one can purchase clicks, likes, or other user interaction. Even the US State Department has been found guilty of buying Facebook "likes" in a fraudulent attempt to boost the perception of the popularity of its Facebook page.[30]

The BOTS Act of 2016

As the industry matures, the body of case law (or legal precedent) continues to expand. However, there are occasions when specific legislation becomes essential. The BOTS Act, officially known as the 'Better Online Ticket Sales Act of 2016,' is a U.S. federal law designed to address the unfair use of automated software or bots to gain access to tickets for events such as concerts, sporting events, and theater performances.

The BOTS Act squarely targets the unfair practices of automated software or bots that swoop in to snatch up tickets as soon as they hit the market. These bots, often wielded by scalpers and ticket resellers, can lead to lightning-fast sell-outs and inflated prices on secondary ticket platforms.

The BOTS Act doesn't outright outlaw ticket resale or

---

29   *What is click fraud? how it works, examples, and red flags.* CHEQ. (2024, January 29). https://cheq.ai/blog/what-is-click-fraud/

30   Ap. (2014, January 6). *How facebook likes get bought and sold.* The Huffington Post. https://web.archive.org/web/20140107005727/http://www.huffingtonpost.com/2014/01/05/buy-facebook-likes_n_4544800.html

automated ticket purchases. Instead, it zeroes in on the misuse of such software. Specifically, it makes it illegal to circumvent control measures put in place to ensure "fair access" to tickets. Moreover, it sternly prohibits the sale of tickets obtained in violation of the act.

While no single case directly triggered the legislation that followed, an Adele tour supposedly cast a spotlight on a pervasive issue: ticket scalping by automated bots. These digital scalpers snapped up large quantities of tickets, leaving genuine fans empty-handed and driving them to pay exorbitant prices on resale platforms.

The purpose of the BOTS Act was to curb the bot-driven frenzy and restore fairness to ticket sales. But did it succeed? The answer lies in the intricate dance between technology and regulation. While the law likely altered the tactics of ticket-buying bots, it's doubtful they ceased their automated shopping sprees altogether. Proving that a ticket was purchased automatically remains a formidable challenge, especially when the buyer willingly accepted the asking price.

Further thoughts

It's important that your competitive intelligence campaigns don't interfere with your subjects operations. The first reason is that you want to avoid legal entanglements when possible. The second reason is more operational. You don't want to affect your subjects operations because it will draw attention to your campaign.

Spying on Success

Chapter 9

Analysis: facts, evidence, and metadata

Your campaigns will collect three types of intelligence: facts, evidence, and metadata. These three types of information are related, but quite different.

This section discusses:

- The definition of "fact"
- How *evidence* is used to calculate the probability of a fact
- How *metadata* can be more valuable than facts
- How bias affects investigations.

Facts

Facts are information that is objectively true and verifiable. Examples of facts include: prices, product names, and employee lists. Some useful things to know about facts include:

- Facts represent information about reality as it exists. As such, facts are not original creations and do not meet the criteria for copyright protection.

- It doesn't matter who knows a fact. Unlike beliefs, facts are nonexclusive. A fact is a fact regardless who believes it, even if no one knows it's a fact.

- Some facts are trade secrets, like the formulas for *Coca-Cola* or *Chanel Number 5*. You can discover and use trade secrets if they are obtained through reverse engineering and observation.

137

- Facts are the basis for evidence.

From a competitive intelligence perspective, it's also important to recognize that facts change. It's not that they expire, but the price recorded today might be different than the price recorded last week. Fluctuating facts are often a source for metadata.

Evidence

Competitive intelligence looks for facts. But when facts aren't available, investigators look for *the evidence of* facts.

Evidence and facts are related. But, there is a distinction. Facts are pieces of information that are accepted as true, while evidence is the broader body of information used to support a particular claim or conclusion.

Evidence is a combination of facts, interpretations, or analyses based on those facts. In legal settings, evidence is presented to persuade and convince, whereas facts are elements of reality that may or may not be disputed.

Often evidence, and not facts, make the best intelligence. If we monitor prices over time, we may see that prices and availability of products fluctuate. Those variabilities are possible evidence of either supply issues or changes in demand. This evidence, on it's own, might not prove anything, but when combined with other collected (and inferred) evidence, it can lead to discovered trade secrets, like: retail strategies, supply chain work-arounds.

Evidence supports the probability of facts

If you possess enough evidence, you can construct a plausible narrative even when you haven't directly observed any of the events.

For instance, consider a woman on her daily commute to work. On the way from her house to her car she steps over a puddle. Without giving it much thought, she concluded that it had rained. As she approached her car, however, she saw the clouds part and the warmth of the morning sun beat comfortably on her shoulders.

"I'm glad it won't rain all day." she thought. "Finally a nice day. It seems to rain every day."

Once settled in her car, she looked through the windscreen. Expecting to see droplets of rain, she instead saw storm clouds retreating to the horizon. "See? I knew it rained." she said to herself.

Anticipating the smell of a recent storm, she closed her eyes and took a deep breath, but smelled nothing. It was only then that she noticed that the grass is wet but the pavement was mostly dry. After first concluding that here had been a storm, she quickly concluded that the irrigation system had run.

In this scenario, the woman's conclusion was drawn not solely from direct facts or observations but from a combination of evidence and her own biases.

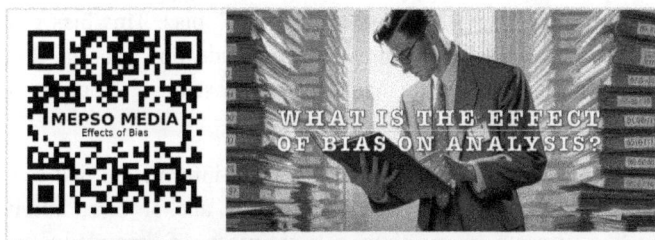

Use QR code to access video, "From Physical to Virtual"

Evidence and bias

Evidence alone can be dangerous. This is because we have a psychological need to satisfy our biases. Our biases affect the way we analyze evidence, as well as facts. These biases are generally formed by undue influence caused by personal experience, stereotypes, or societal pressure. When left unchecked, our biases filter our ability to think. Biases adversely affect decisions, perceptions, and judgements, with an obvious affect on outcomes.

Bias is a powerful force. After all, many millions of dollars are spent to influence the biases of customers toward one product and away from another.

The best data analysts often are the ones who have identified and dealt with their own natural biases.

Types of Bias

Proper analysis of evidence is nearly impossible when the evidence is first filtered by the biases of the analyst. So let's take a moment to examine a few of the most common types of bias in hope that it makes our own personal biases easier to identify.

- *Anchor Bias* is when there is a preference for the first solution to a problem. You could say that this is a, "We've always done it that way." bias. This bias can be solved by implementing an ideation process that requires more than one proposed solution to a problem.

- *Proximity Bias* is a preference to information that was last encountered. It's similar to anchor bias, but it repeats every time a new piece of knowledge is acquired. People with this bias tend to follow, not lead, trends.

- *Cognitive Bias* gives a preference to information that is readily available or easily recalled. Sometimes this bias is also known as *Availability Bias*. The idiom, "When your only tool is a hammer, every problem is a nail." applies here. This bias is a lazy habit that can also be solved by a process that requires multiple pieces of evidence before a conclusion is reached.

* *Confirmation Bias* refers to the tendency to favor information that confirms or supports a pre-existing belief. People with confirmation bias dismiss facts that contradict personal beliefs. This bias is a lifestyle bias. For example, a naturally optimistic person may ignore negative news because it has no place in their worldview. Likewise, people tend to consume news and attract friends that don't challenge their political opinions.

* *Emotional Bias* is a preference for either positive or negative outcomes. This bias can be exhibited by overly upbeat management, who insist on positivity. Or, if you constantly need to "see the good in people", you have fallen victim to this bias. Actively seeking negative outcomes is often the result of *gaslighting,* or manipulating people into believing that their situation is hopeless.

* *Social Bias* is a preference toward being members of favored social groups. For example, the survey question: *"Do you always recycle to save the environment?"* encourages the respondent to answer with a social bias to the affirmative. Social biases tend to be more aspirational than an accurate reflections of status.

* *Decision-making Bias* is when one overestimates their problem solving ability. It is also closely related to *The Dunning–Kruger effect*, which is a cognitive bias where people don't understand the limitations of their own thinking or abilities. Decision-making bias is a common contributor to feature creep, described earlier.

* *Overconfidence Bias* is when we continue to make

decisions based on prior successes, even when it is not rational to do so. This is a particularly dangerous bias to have in rapidly changing environments.

- *Conformity Bias* defines our need to fit in. This isn't always a bad bias when it encourages conformance to procedure and policy. But unfortunately, conformity bias also encourages *hive think*, or *the susceptibility of a group of people to think alike*.

- *Attribution Bias* describes the condition when someone takes all the credit for successes while attributing all failures to others. This bias is also known as *Self-serving Bias* and *Self-enhancement Bias*. In either case, this is not a good bias for a data analyst to have.

The nature of bias

Biases are distortions of facts; and they're everywhere. Human history is written with the bias of conquerors. For example, you'll find very few accounts of the colonization of the Americas not told by Europeans. Bias is an emotional reaction to a situation, frequently used to subconsciously hide agendas, sometimes our own, and sometimes those belonging to others.

It's important to know that we all prejudge situations and that prejudice is the antitheses of analysis. Adding names and descriptions to these biases, as we just did, will hopefully help you identify your biases before they result in poor analysis.

Real-world bias

Biases distort the expertise of even professional inspectors; sometimes with life and death consequences. This is what happened in the murder and arson case of a poor young man a few years ago.[31]

Cameron Willingham was a man in his early twenties. He was married with three young children. They lived in a trailer park in rural Texas. His wife and three children died in a residential fire.

Willingham's recognition of the tragedy was that the heat of the fire woke him from his sleep. He said that his first instinct was to run to the bedroom, where his children were sleeping. In sworn testimony, he stated that the heat was so intense that his hair started to singe when he entered their room. Realizing that the heat would prevent him from rescuing anyone, including himself, he ran down the hallway to the front door where he screamed to his neighbors for help.

After the fire, professional fire investigators were summoned to examine the evidence. Fire investigators typically start their investigations where the fire damage is the worst because this is likely where the fire started. The most severe damage was in the hallway that led from the back bedroom, where the children slept, to the front door. The investigators identified what looked like pools and splash marks in the hallway. They interpreted these marks as sure signs that an accelerant, like gasoline, had been applied to the floor. Also on the walls, were classic "V" shaped patterns of smoke. These were in agreement with how fires normally spread from the floor to the walls and finally the ceiling.

The issue of whether or not an accelerant was used was essential to the case against Willingham. If an accelerant was used it would prove intent. And if the fire was by caused by arson, there would also be additional murder or man slaughter charges.

---

[31] *Cameron Todd Willingham: Wrongfully convicted and executed in Texas.* Innocence Project. (2023, May 2). https://innocenceproject.org/cameron-todd-willingham-wrongfully-convicted-and-executed-in-texas

The investigators were struck by three particularly interesting pieces of evidence. One of these was a pane of glass with a spider pattern of fine cracks. These patterns lead the investigators to believe that the fire was exceptionally hot, again, showing signs that an accelerant had been used.

Another key piece of evidence was the front door. This door had an aluminum threshold meant to protect the floor below. But the floor below the door's threshold was charred. This, to the investigators, was more evidence that an accelerant was used because temperatures in a natural fire would not have grown hot enough to char the wood beneath the threshold.

The last piece of evidence came when Willingham was examined, and they saw that his feet were unburned. They wondered how his feet could have remained unburned if he had exited the bedroom through the hallway where the fire had started. They concluded that it was more probable that he spread the accelerant, lit the fire, and ran out the front door.

Ultimately, Willingham was convicted of murdering his wife and three children. Since there were more than three victims, the case became an automatic death penalty sentence under Texas law. He was, however, offered life in prison if he pled guilty to the crimes. But he testified that he was innocent, and that he'd rather die than falsely admit to killing his family. He was eventually executed.

Years later, another forensic investigator took a look at the evidence of this fire. Unlike the original investigators, this man conducted bias-free experiments to recreate conditions that either cause fires, or happen during fires.

This investigator conducted experiments that proved that when fires build quickly, they are apt to leave marks that look like the spill and pooling marks left by accelerants. Additionally, he looked at the spider pattern in the glass, that the earlier investigators saw as evidence of an excessively hot fire. Unlike the earlier investigators, he was unable to conclude that the pattern in the glass hadn't existed before the fire. The new investigator also conducted experiments that proved that the charred floor beneath the door threshold was predictable for non-accelerant fires.

Consequently, if no accelerant was used, the hallway wouldn't have been subject to the burning gasoline (or whatever accelerant was supposedly used) and the convicted man's feet would not have been burned, as was the case.

While he didn't state what actually started the fire, the new investigator ruled out arson as the cause. Since this shouldn't have been classified as an arson case, the probability is high that the biases of the first investigators led to killing an innocent man.

This story shows the importance of the quality of investigator training. In many places, one can become a fire investigator after only 40 hours of instruction. *(Incidentally, one can become a competitive intelligence expert without any qualifications whatsoever!)*

Often, young investigators are paired with a more experienced investigator. This might be a good way for an expert to share experience with an apprentice. But learning this way is also leads to older examiners spreading biases to new investigators.

While competitive intelligence seldom involves life and death matters, the consequences of misreading evidence can be expensive.

Bias is baked-in

Probably the most important takeaway from this discussion of bias is that we all exhibit bias of some type. It's part of our DNA. Our evolution was largely dependent on fight or flight responses to our environment. Those same factors are triggered today when we are put in stressful situations. But unlike yesterday, when a flight response was the difference between a nice day and getting eaten by a predator, these responses aren't useful in analysis. Hopefully, knowing your biases will help you better evaluate your own decision making ability.

Artificial intelligence and Bias

It's important to remember that artificial intelligence inherits the biases of that which it was trained on. For that matter, it's sometimes important to know the era and locale of the sourced data. The other area where artificial intelligence may appear to show a bias is when it hallucinates, or provides information that appears to be valid, when in fact is a total fabrication.

Metadata

Metadata is one of the most misunderstood and valuable types of information. There's much to know about metadata, but perhaps the most important things to remember are:

- Metadata gives data context
- When metadata does not exist naturally, it can be created.

Use QR code to access video, "What is Metadata?"

Parametric metadata

Early adopters of digital photography learned about metadata with the introduction of *XIF*, or the *Extended Image File Format*. These pieces of metadata were embedded into image

146

files and provided information related to the photo, like: the geo-coordinates of where the photo was taken, the f-stop used by the camera, and the date of creation. While the XIF data wasn't the actual photograph, it provided context for the image.

Created metadata

Metadata is often the outcome of analysis. For example, if you collect prices for the identical product two weeks apart, the difference between those two prices is metadata, so is the direction of change. In this case, this metadata might be called something like $PriceChange^{Weekly}$. The direction of change could be called $PriceChange^{Trend}$. Again, this created metadata is often more valuable than the collected prices without metadata.

Metadata in pop culture

Many of us became aware of metadata after *Edward Snowden* violated the *Espionage Act of 1917* and released documents describing the *NSA PRISM* surveillance program.

While Snowden leaked a massive amount of information, it was largely the term "metadata" that piqued the public's interest. This sudden interest in metadata was triggered when US citizens learned that the United States government was secretly collecting metadata on their phone conversations.

At the time, the vast majority of US citizens weren't sure what metadata was, but once the public caught wind that they were subject to warrantless surveillance, citizens demanded to know more about metadata.

In the wake of the Snowden disclosures, the Senate Intelligence Committee called a hurried meeting to deal with the fallout of the leak. One of the first members to be interviewed after the meeting was California Senator Dianne Feinstein. She engaged the press and tried to put the public's tensions to rest. The

147

interview started poorly, after admitting that she didn't know what a *database query* was, she said,

> *"As you know, this is just metadata. There's no content involved."[32]*

While this statement was technically correct, it probably did more to raise questions than settle nerves. After all, it's difficult to relax knowing that it's *"just metadata"* when you're not quite sure what metadata is to begin with. More importantly, there is a sense that the value of metadata was intentionally diminished.

While Dianne Feinstein's explanation failed to identify the importance of metadata, the former NSA Chief, Michael Hayden made the importance of metadata clear, when he said,

> *"We kill people over Metadata."[33]*

The reality is that Senator Feinstein was actually correct. The metadata that was collected contained no content. Metadata merely provided context of phone calls that had been made.

Perhaps the best way to understand the power of metadata is to see how the United States was using metadata to monitor it's own citizens.

How metadata is made

Metadata was used heavily in The United States by the *National Security Administration, or NSA*, through the authorization of the *PATRIOT Act*. This set of laws was a reaction to the *9/11 attacks* and allowed government agencies to collect information on phone calls.

---

[32]   Reeve, E. (2022, May 12). *Washington is trapped in its own prism of data-mining self-defense.* The Atlantic. https://www.theatlantic.com/politics/archive/2013/06/nsa-prism-defense-analysis/314480/

[33]   ABC News Network. (n.d.). ABC News. https://abcnews.go.com/blogs/headlines/2014/05/ex-nsa-chief-we-kill-people-based-on-metadata

As mentioned earlier, metadata is used to create context for intelligence. This was particularly handy for the NSA, because they really didn't want to know specifically what people were saying in phone conversations. That level of intelligence would require search warrants for each of the millions and millions of phone conversations they planned to monitor. From a process standpoint, they would not have been able to monitor that many conversations without using metadata. But by relying on metadata, the NSA was able to filter probable crimes from normal conversations, and focus their attention on serious problems.

The NSA actually collected very little information. They only recoded the following metadata:

1. The originating phone number
2. The phone numbers of everyone in the call
3. The time and duration of the call.

This doesn't sound like a lot of information. But these three parameters were enough to profile individuals of interest. For example:

- People generally communicate within the same groups. So, the NSA metadata could be used to identify groups of people that were associated in some way.

- Phone calls that happen regularly indicate some type of organization.

- Calls that precede or follow specific events can be correlated with the event. There is usually a lot of chatter leading up to security events.

- Short phone calls that routinely call the same phone number at regular intervals may reflect subordinates checking in with a superior.

- If one phone number regularly calls the same set of numbers, that originating number probably belongs to someone managing others.

- If phone numbers are associated with cell phones, the numbers are more *personally identifying* than a landline number. Additionally, a callers rough location can be triangulated with cell tower logs.

- Calls made to or from foreign phone numbers (or satellite phones) gathered more attention than domestic calls.

- Once statistical patterns are established, analysts can start looking at anomalies, or outlaying data, to discover the use of burner phones, or other suspicious activity.

If there was a specific phone call, or more probably a collection of phone calls, that the NSA believed contained information of national importance, they would file a request with the FISA Court. This court would determine if the data indicated a threat that warranted further investigation.

Metadata allowed the NSA to establish profiles, and then investigate those profiles that are deemed to be potentially dangerous. But not every profile is sinister. For example, if there is a call from a residential landline to a business number every Monday through Friday at roughly 3:15pm, it may be a child calling a parent to inform that they are home from school.

It's important to note that the effectiveness of such profiling depends on the scale of the metadata collection, the quality of the analysis tools, and the specific goals of intelligence agencies. Additionally, the collection and analysis of this metadata was controversial due to concerns about privacy, civil liberties, and the potential for abuse.

There is always metadata

No matter the intelligence that's collected, there is always metadata that can be created. Perhaps the simplest metadata is the found intelligence combined with the date on which it was collected. This is useful because metadata puts data in context and time is a great orientation tool.

Anytime you attach a timestamp to something, you orient the collected data with time. Once you have a statistically relevant collection of these data/timestamp pairs, you may be able to detect historic patterns. These patterns should allow for projections of how you predict data will look in the future. This is particularly useful when tracking prices, but can also be applied to any organizational inputs or outputs.

Examples of metadata:
- The time when data was acquired
- The place data was acquired
- The organization acquiring the intelligence
- The direction of change
- The relationship to other data, like: the *rate of sales*
- The amount of time required to do something
- When something was there but is now gone,
- Rate relationships, for example, occupancy rates

Other uses for metadata

Metadata can be used to create a hierarchy of data, to group related data together, and to make it easier to find specific pieces of data. For example, a library might use metadata to organize its books by author, title, and genre. Library Science uses such metadata to make document retrieval easier; because it would be impossible to organize books based on their entire content. That's also what the NSA learned, and why they found metadata to be so useful.

As described, metadata can be used to improve the discoverability of data. When data is properly tagged with metadata, it can be more easily found by search engines and other applications.

Further thoughts

You can't effectively analyze evidence if your personal biases are out of control. It's OK to have a bias. We all do. But it is paramount that we don't let biases rule your thinking process. The best way to limit the effect of bias is to identify, not just personal biases, but the biases of your organization and industry.

Correcting your biases will result in better analysis. And, detecting the biases of your industry may reveal opportunities.

Chapter 10
Finding sources

Your sources are the most important part of your competitive intelligence campaign. This chapter looks at where to find sources and how to treat them once you decide to use them. We will also explore both private and *OSINT*, or Open Source Intelligence sources

OSINT

Most, but not all of the sources described in this chapter are public, but that doesn't mean they are pedestrian or in anyway incapable of creating reams of metadata. The key is to approach your sources as someone other than the primary audience. Look for unintended communications that are overlooked by people consuming the intended content.

How to treat sources

You've read this before, I'm repeating myself for emphasis.

> *Treat your sources with the upmost respect.*
> *Don't do anything that draws attention to*
> *your campaign.*

Be kind to both private and public sources. The golden rule of competitive intelligence is to touch your resources as little as possible. You don't want to draw unwarranted attention to yourself. Your campaigns are trade secrets. And once they are discovered; they are lost.

Tips for staying stealthy

Here are a few tips for ensuring the privacy of your campaigns, especially if your using bots.

- Don't work too quickly. Bots can operate much faster than any human. Use software "throttles" to regulate how quickly your bots perform. Recognize that there is a minimal amount of time required to download and consume a webpage or to complete and submit a form. Don't rush!

- Randomize your behavior. In addition to not working too quickly, you don't want your bot to perform functions exactly one second apart. Random delays should be regularly inserted into your process. Additionally, your bot or process shouldn't take the same path every time.

- Run campaigns during regular working hours when traffic patterns are high. Running campaigns during times of peak traffic reduces the possibility that your interactions stand out. Avoid running campaigns during quiet times and you'll reduce of odds of encountering system performance issues caused by routine maintenance.

Anonymity is immediately lost when you, or your bot, log into a private or paid data source. This becomes an issue if your campaign does something stupid. Because now, not only have you brought attention to your campaign, but now the source can also trace the activity back to you. If you need to access a lot of data, you might consider coordinating your collection over multiple accounts.

Obstacles and interference

Many of the good sources, public and private, realize they are prime sources of competitive intelligence. Because of this, they are often designed to be difficult to use. A common tactic is to only allow access to.a small portion of the total report. Or maybe, the source requires that you repetitively complete redundant questions before requesting a report.

As you may have guessed, bots are better able to cope with these limitations than human investigators.

The best known obstacle used to separate you from your intelligence source is the CAPTCHA, which is used to authenticate users. Sources will also use CAPTCHAs as *throttles* to slow the rate at which you download pages from the website.

Realistically, CAPTCHAs do little to keep bots from accessing data. In fact, my last book[34] has a entire chapter devoted to automatically solving CAPTCHAs.

(Note: If you have the right to access data and services there is nothing inherently wrong with automatically solving a CAPTCHA.)

Search engines

The first search engines were essentially lists of FTP servers. It wasn't until 1991 when the first search engine for webpages, W3Catalog, became available. Once people discovered that they could sell advertising in searches, it started a proliferation of search engines like: AltaVista, Lycos, Yahoo!, WebCrawler, MSN Search, Inktomi, and BackRub, which later became Google.

Google quickly became the main player and consolidation quickly followed. Today Google has over 91% of the search market, with Bing in second place with fewer than 4%.

The casualty of search consolidation is the lack of diversity in search results. There was a day when AltaVista returned different search results than Lycos or *Yahoo!* But now the

---

[34] Michael Schrenk, *"Developing Bots with Selenium Python"*, 2023, Mepso Media, Las Vegas

remaining search engines return very similar results. Much of the search results you see today come from the same source, regardless of the search engine you're using.

Global search engines

If you look outside of the English speaking world, you can find new search opportunities in the global search market. Additionally, many of these search companies also provide other services, like email and hosting.

Country	URL	Origin	Notes
China	baidu.com	1999	One of the world's largest Internet and AI companies.
Japan	goo.jp	2003	Tokyo, Japan
Slovenia	najdi.si	2004	Ljubljana, Slovienia
Russia	yandex.ru	1994	Moscow, Russia
	yandex.com	1998	Hosted in Florida
Sweden	eniro.se	1986	Hosted in California
S. Korea	naver.com	1997	Seongnam, Korea
Poland	onet.pl	1990	Hosted in California
France	orange.fr	2006	Paris, France
Iran	parseek.com	2002	Hosted in California
Portugal	sapo.pt	2002	Porto, Portugal
Switzerland	search.se	2022	More English-centric than you'd expect.
Czech Rep.	seznam.cz	2007	Hosted in Germany
Israel	walla.co.il	Unknown	Hosted in California

International search engines

International search engines are useful even if you don't speak the native language because modern browsers have the ability to translate languages. Additionally, these search engines often draw from sources that are different than the English-centric search companies.

Automating searches

You may be tempted to run bots that perform automated searches. I don't have a lot of experience in this area because I've learned that search engines don't like being automated.

This is particularly true of Google. I have tried to determine how they detect bots, but they're so good at it that I have stopped trying. If you attempt to automate search, go very slowly, use lots of IP addresses, and maybe your bot can do something useful before it's shut down. But I generally don't recommend automated tactics on search engines.

The semantic web

The language of the web is HTML, or the *Hypertext Markup Language*. HTML intermixes content with formatting controls. While it's easy for a person to visually pick-out the content on a rendered webpage, it is more difficult for a bot to parse an HTML page. It can be done, it's just a little more difficult.

Tim Berners-Lee, the creator of the World Wide Web, envisioned development of a *semantic web,* where the webpage describes the nuances of the content, not the display format. The semantic web is machine readable and the content can be formatted in whatever way required by the requesting platform.

The semantic web was a great idea that never caught on. Perhaps the problem was that the semantic web was introduced well before the proliferation of cellphones and tablets, which would most benefit from it's use. However, the affects of the semantic web have have led to implementations at a smaller scale. One of those smaller scale successes is *RSS,* or *Really Simple Syndication*[35]. RSS is the standard that is used to distribute news and data-feeds to webmasters.

---

[35] Or less often known as, Rich Site Summary.

The following figure depicts a typical RSS file. Notice how the <tags> </tags> are used to describe the content. This style of formatting is optimized for machine reading.

```
<?xml version="1.0" encoding="UTF-8"?>
<rss version="2.0">
 <channel>
  <title>RSS Example</title>
  <link>https://www.mylink.com</link>
  <description>Stay updated with the latest news!</description>
  <item>
   <title>Latest News</title>
   <link>https://www.mylink.com/latestNews</link>
   <description>Check out our latest news!</description>
   <pubDate>Thu, 04 Apr 2024 08:00:00 GMT</pubDate>
  </item>
  <item>
   <title>Previous Stories</title>
   <link>https://www.mylink.com/previousNews</link>
   <description>Check out our previous stories</description>
   <pubDate>Thu, 04 Apr 2024 08:00:00 GMT</pubDate>
  </item>
  <!-- Add more items here -->
 </channel>
</rss>
```

A sample RSS file

Today, there are frequently updated RSS feeds for basically any information you want to research.

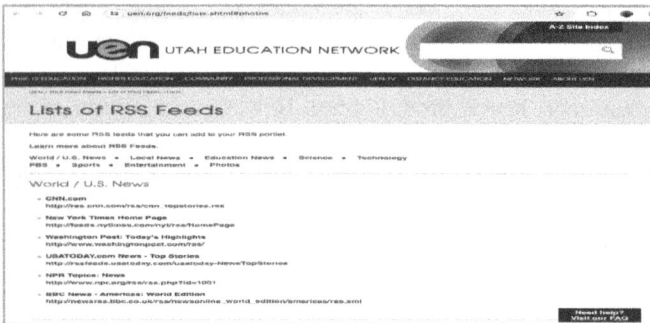

One of many RSS sources

An example of an RSS aggregator is shown above. Today RSS feeds are mostly used to syndicate information on websites. But they can also be used for competitive intelligence purposes.

Finance

There are multiple sources for Financial data in RSS format. If you use one of these sources be aware that the data is usually delayed. This is important if you expect the data to be timely. For example, if you are using this information to do day-trading, know that large institutions pay exorbitant sums of money for financial data that isn't delayed. So if you're using online financial data in this way you are the victim of competitive intelligence. In other words, if you're day-trading based on the data you get from Yahoo Finance, you're a bit out of your league.

There is, however, a lot of financial data available if your competitive intelligence applications need it. If you don't need by-the-microsecond updates, you'll certainly find a RSS source that meets your needs. Some of the more useful metrics to collect might include:

- Currency prices
- Interest rates (both paid and assessed)
- Bond rates
- Housing (days on market, etc.)
- The Consumer Confidence Index
- Various commodity prices.

Financial data are facts. These facts are useful in the creation of metadata. For example, you can create very specific metrics. For example, metadata like *SalesPerGDP* could provide insights as to how your organization ranks against the economy at large.

Government publications

Government publications are a primary source for authoritative information. Whether "authoritative" equates to "truth" is a matter of the government selected. But in any case, it is the authentic voice of the government.

In the United States, all government publications are in the public domain. So you can use them as you see fit. This includes vast volumes of information from *NASA*, The *National Aeronautics and Space Administration*[36], including imagery. If you need climatic data of any kind, you'll find outstanding information at *NOAA*, or The *National Oceanic and Atmospheric Administration*[37].

Another office of particular interest is the *United States Office of Patents and Trademarks*[38], or the *USPTO*. Their website makes it easy to search on competitor names or other keywords.

Another important office is the US Department of State[39]. In addition to issuing passports and maintaining international relations, the State Department also publishes staggering amounts of international demographic data. I've also found their traveler safety warnings particularly useful.

The Unites States Census Bureau[40] also publishes a trove of useful demographic data. In addition to detailed domestic US demographic information, the Census Bureau also publishes reports on:
- Economics
- Housing
- Education
- Health.

---

[36] NASA, National Aeronautics and Space Administration. https://www.nasa.gov/

[37] NOAA, National Oceanic and Atmospheric Administration. https://www.noaa.gov/

[38] USPTO, United States Patent and Trademark Office. https://www.uspto.gov/

[39] U. S. Department of State. https://www.state.gov/

[40] U. S. Census Bureau. http://www.census.gov/

Think global and local

The nice thing about government publications is that you have a world's worth to choose from. Europe, Asia, Africa, and Australia all have governmental websites worth exploring.

Local governments also have regulations and reporting policies that potentially reveal competitive intelligence. One such example is California's *Worker Adjustment and Retraining Notification* program, or WARN. Under this law, employers must publicly announce layoffs and plant closings sixty days in advance. The intent of the law is to give workers time to adjust to pending layoffs or plant closings. To an investigator, however, the unintended communication is that a potential competitor is doing major organizational restructuring that becomes effective in two months.

Surveys

One way to find out what people think is to ask them though surveys. Unfortunately, surveys have lost much of their appeal. Much of this is due to the massive number of surveys we're each exposed to. Another adverse factor is the heightened awareness of personal privacy.

Self-selected groups

One aspect of surveys is that they almost always source from self-selected groups. For example, if you're working with reviews from a website like yelp.com or tripadvisor.com those reviews are from people, who were motivated to write a review. The people, who didn't leave a review, are not included in the survey. This has the tendency to amplify extreme opinions.

It's always important to know that there are many more people, who failed to leave a review, probably because they didn't feel obligated to do so.

When sampling is unscientific opinions have little real

statistical value. They can, however, show trends of those that participate.

It is not as easy to conduct *Survey Science* as it once was. In the past, researchers used phone book data to find statistically significant samples, based on demographics. Not only are phone books no longer distributed, but many people, myself included, move and keep their cellphone number, making area codes poor locators.

Bias and surveys

You explored biases earlier in this section. There you learned that biases can destroy the analysis phase of investigations. In addition to bad analysis, biases can also produce bad procedures. This may be most evident in poorly constructed surveys; where survey questions are formed from the investigator's biases. Some common examples are shown below.

Leading questions are those that anticipate a specific answer for example, "Do you agree that there's nothing like a hot cup of coffee in the morning?" directly injects the questioner's personal bias toward a good morning coffee into the survey.

Loaded questions are those the force the respondent to agree with you. For example, "Do you like the customer service at our amazing company?" In this case, the respondent is agreeing that the company is amazing, regardless how they feel about the customer service.

Double-barreled questions are those that demand that the respondence provide two answers in one response. A question like, "Do you approve of our new safety plans and the way they were implemented?" is really two questions and deserves two responses.

Vague questions are questions that are so unspecific that they produce unusable responses. For example, consider the

164

following questions and notice the italicized words.

"Did you *enjoy* the event?"
"How *satisfied* are you with our service"
"Do you think our policies are *fair*?"

Each of the italicized words above, voice a second level of interpretation that are not incorporated into the question. As shown in the example above, your expectations for an enjoyable event may be very different than someone else's.

The Likert scale

You can avoid confusion in surveys by using *The Likert scale*, which is a question followed by an odd number responses that range from very affirmative to very negative, with a neutral stop in the middle. A Likert scale survey question might take the following form.

> *On a scale from 1 to 5, how would you rate your parasailing adventure:*
>
> 1. *Very bad*
> 2. *Mostly bad*
> 3. *Neither good nor bad*
> 4. *Mostly good*
> 5. *Very good*

In Likert scale survey questions, it's important not to inject bias into questions, so it's important not to use words that can be interpreted several ways. So, it would be inadvisable to use response scales with descriptions like the following:

> *On a scale from 1 to 5, how would you rate your parasailing adventure:*
>
> 1. *Terrifying*
> 2. *Pretty scary*
> 3. *Boring*
> 4. *Invigorating*

5. *Caught a good thrill*

This second survey question won't be as effective as the first because there are too many ways to interpret the scale.

The other aspect of using the Likert scale is that the resulting data is very easy for both a person or a machine to interpret and gauge. It's best to limit your scale to three or five choices. Any more than that and people start to have problems differentiating the difference between their options. People don't naturally put things on a scale of one to ten unless forced to. If you use more than five options you'll get a lot of responses on either end and in the middle of the scale.

QR codes as surveys

This book makes use of *QR codes*, or *Quick Response codes*. They are those square barcodes you've seen everywhere from print advertisements to Television Screens. An example is shown below

A QR, or Quick Response Code, redirects to www.mepso.com

QR codes have been around for a long time but only became common during the Covid pandemic. During that period, many restaurants stopped using menus. Instead they provided QR codes that provided easy access to their online menu from cell phones.

Affixed QR codes

When QR codes are affixed to a surface, one obtains an opportunity to find web surfers based on a physical location. This is a much more accurate way to pinpoint to location of web servers than geolocating through IP addresses. These QR codes can also be applied to semi-fixed objects like restaurant menus. As an example, a restaurant chain uses a QR code to access the online menu from all of their locations. Every time someone accesses the menu, they leave behind the same trail of information anyone else leaves when they use a website. With this scant amount of information, an investigator could find ways to estimate:

- Which restaurants had the most traffic?

- How long do people wait for service?

- What is the average number of times someone checks the menu?

- Are customers using the entire menu?

If the website, on the other side of the QR code, was also used for food selection and payment, there would be a trove of intelligence that could be applied to product selection, pricing, scheduling, etc.

Mobile QR codes

The interesting thing about QR codes is that they don't have to stay in one place. For example, placing a QR code during a televised documentary, or on the side of a truck, provides a new set of metrics.

For example, one way to test the viability of a product would be to publish information about your product on billboards around the country. If those billboards had tagged QR codes, or QR codes that lead the user to a specific page on a server that tagged it's source, you would be able to gauge interest, in realtime.

In another idea, if you have large inventory that is spread around a store or a lot, you could create QR codes for each piece of merchandise, providing product details. As customer's scan the QR codes, the log files that receive the QR requests for webpages could effectively create a heat map that physically shows if your store layout is in agreement to where customers think their time is best spent.

Surveilling online stores

Many of the larger competitive intelligence projects I've taken on have involved monitoring online stores. The important thing to remember about online stores is that with only a product description and a price, one is able to deduce a remarkable amount of intelligence. Here's a standard list of intelligence you can get from just those few parameters.

- The most obvious thing to do is to compare this price with your own to create a piece of metadata that is the price difference between your price and theirs.

  - The magnitude of this value indicates if your price is higher or lower than their price.

  - Once you collect this price for multiple vendors, you can create an AverageMarketPrice. (Your price should be excluded from this value).

  - Keep in mind that a constant effort to match prices will result in what I call the race to the bottom with no winners. Your strategies should also look for times when you can competitively raise prices.

- As you collect this data periodically, you can start to see pricing trends. With enough history, you should be able to predict future prices with some accuracy.

  - If one day the product doesn't appear where it was, we can assume that this product is out of stock.

- When the product reappears, we can count the number of days it was out of stock, ie: DaysOutOfStock.

- When other vendors also report that the item is out of stock, it can reflect supplier or supply chain issues.

- When groups of products are missing from catalogs at the same time, it can reflect some type of grouping, perhaps through suppliers or supply chain.

- When new products appear, with no price history, it probably indicates an expansion to their product line. And conversely, when a product disappears it has probably been discontinued.

- What conclusions can be made about the products, whose price changes the most frequently?

  - What can we conclude about products whose prices never change?

  - Do price changes happen at an incremental level or do sweeping price changes happen all at once?

- What does it mean when product descriptions are rewritten?

- Is there anything about your competitor's habits that show they are following your lead?

The amount of intelligence that can be gleaned from online stores is massive, and it grows when specific applications are met. For example, in some markets, where you can positively identify items (like real estate and automobiles) there is enough information available that you have almost as much available intelligence as the source's Accounts Receivable department.

Private marketplaces

One of my favorite sources for intelligence are private marketplaces like eBay and Etsy. These marketplaces facilitate trade between buyers and independent sellers. While they both started small; eBay transacts of $70 billion annually[41], and while not as large, Etsy still manages to facilitate nearly $3 billion in annual sales[42]. While these may be the two largest players in this area, there are many more niche markets services by marketplaces like these. Just remember that the source needs sufficient sales to be statistically relevant.

In the past, these marketplaces have been an unusually rich area for retail intelligence.

Social Media

Platforms like Twitter, Facebook, LinkedIn, Instagram, and others provide a wealth of information about individuals, organizations, events, and trends. Users often share personal and professional details that can be valuable for OPSEC purposes.

Social media as a source of statistics

Much of the intelligence found on Social Media lacks the statistical integrity to make it useful. Some of the things that work against social media becoming a great source for intelligence include:

- Participants of social media are all members of self-selected groups.

- Many participants of social media are not human. These automated accounts do not reflect normal

[41] Statista Research Department, & 28, F. (2023, February 28). *eBay gross merchandising volume GMV 2022*. Statista. https://www.statista.com/statistics/242276/ebays-fixed-price-trading-as-share-of-total-gross-merchandise-volume/

[42] *Etsy revenue 2013-2023: Etsy*. Macrotrends. (n.d.). https://www.macrotrends.net/stocks/charts/ETSY/etsy/revenue

human activity or opinions.

- Private posts also affect the accessibility of data harvested from social media.

Understanding the business of social media

While I've found little intelligence value in social media, if your *business is social media*, you may benefit from collecting metrics concerning advertising and content strategies that are found on the various platforms.

A couple of resources you might want to tap include the socialblade.com website, as shown below.

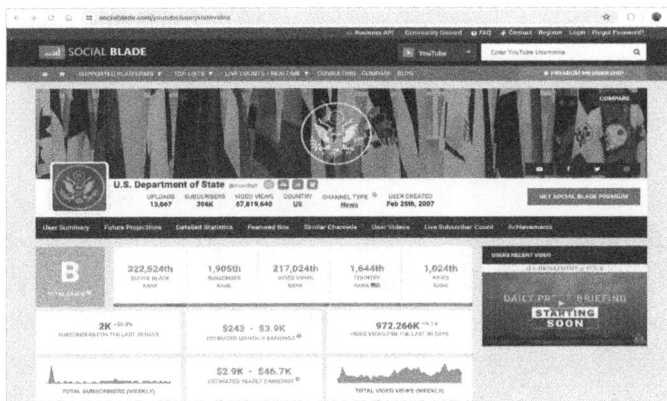

Monitoring social media: SocialBlade.com

This website offers contemporary and historic metrics for most of the major contributors on most popular social media platforms.

If there's an influencer that you'd like to study whom they're not monitoring, you can ask SocialBlade to include them.

Problems with social media

I haven't found any good tools for mining social media data. I suspect that is because outside of marketing, of which I do little, there is little competitive intelligence data on social media. Additionally, the number of bots that use social media for political purposes destroys the statistical value of the data.

The other problem with social media is that much of it is private. One trick you might find useful is to see if any of your private posts have been mistakenly labeled as public. If you want to search what anyone said publicly on Facebook, you could write a Google search term like the following.

```
site:facebook.com "screenName"
```

Searching for public comments on social media

The search query above should find any public Facebook comments associated with the selected screen name.

LinkedIn

LinkedIn.com boasts being, "The world's largest professional network on the Internet"[43]. But in reality, it is social media. And as such it inherits all the privacy issues of that medium.

According to Louis Camassa[44], of the brand consulting company EMPATH, LinkedIn is the social media website where Fortune 500 decision makers spend their time. He also claimed that 80% of B2B leads are generated on LinkedIn. This gives LinkedIn it's value. It's probably why Microsoft paid

---

[43] *What is LinkedIn and how can I use it* https://www.linkedin.com/help/linkedin/answer/a548441/what-is-linkedin-and-how-can-i-use-it-

[44] DeVries, H. (2018, November 16). *The Best Social Media for Lead Generation*. Forbes. https://www.forbes.com/sites/henrydevries/2018/11/16/the-best-social-media-for-lead-generation

$26.2 billion for the company[45], making LinkedIn it's biggest acquisition to date.

It's hard to believe but before LinkedIn, employee lists were trade secrets. Employers didn't want competitors to know who was on the teams they built. Additionally, they certainly didn't want their specific skills disclosed. Today, it would be very difficult to keep an employee list private as they are all published on LinkedIn.

The consequences of having ready access to everyone's resumes and employment status should be obvious to you by this point. It would be easy for a talent recruiter to develop a bot (or develop a systematic way of doing this by hand) to scan LinkedIn and record the people who work in a specific industry. After a few scans, you'll be able to:

- Statistically, determine how often people change jobs within this industry.

    - With the age of the candidate, calculate the rate of job change per stage of their career.

    - Using the information above, calculate which potential candidates are most likely to be looking for new employment.

- Identify employees, whose status has gone from "employed" to "open to opportunities".

- Identify people to claim to have accepted new positions. Plot a heat map with this information to find hot employment regions and employers.

Those are a few ideas. You're only limited to your own creativity. There are many more metrics that can be used to create metadata, including:

- The frequency that people update their profiles

---

[45] Alspach, K. (n.d.). *Microsoft to acquire LinkedIn for $26.2B*. CRN. https://www.crn.com/news/cloud/300081013/microsoft-to-acquire-linkedin-for-26-2b

- Who has multiple profiles?
- The amount of content their profile has
- How often they mention their employer.

LinkedIn = LeakedOut

When people post to LinkedIn, they retain the rights to their contributions. But that doesn't say that they have the rights to publish everything they know. There have been multiple reports of people leaking highly sensitive information on LinkedIn.

Email harvesting

In 2021, an enterprising hacker was able to capture 700 million email addresses, and other *PPI*, or *personally identifying information*[46] from LinkedIn by performing simple web scraping and a little analysis.

Email addresses are easy to guess once you've unlocked the method of assigning email addresses. Today, the standard for corporate email addresses appears to be:

```
(firstInitial + lastName) @ organization.com
```

When organizations standardize on email address that are based on actual names, the email addresses become very easy to guess. If your organization has a policy of assigning email addresses with a set convention, of any type, you need to be careful of publishing employee names.

I once had a client who published a monthly employee newsletter to their corporate website. Within the month of publishing an article about the CEO's executive assistant, and mentioning both her first and last names, she received several authentic-looking but fake emails, or phishing attempts, from the CEO, asking her to wire cash to specific accounts. In one

---

[46] *LinkedIn data leak exposes 700 million users.* Trend Micro News. (2022, October 14). https://news.trendmicro.com/2021/04/27/reported-linkedin-data-breach-what-you-need-to-know/

case, she nearly wired several thousand dollars to one of these social hackers.

This is also a reminder that the greatest threat to any security system is the people who use it. And security tools will not fix human errors.

Ethical concerns over LinkedIn use

At least here in the US, employers are not allowed to infringe on employee free speech and cannot curtail social media use. But, employers are also not obligated to employ employees after they violate nondisclosure agreements signed at the time of employment.

I highly suggest that employers specifically review their LinkedIn policies and educate their employees on the difference between their right to post personal information in public places, and their obligation to keep organizational secrets.

LinkedIn and espionage

More than C-Suite executives read LinkedIn. The social media site has also become a place to find potential espionage partners. In one famous case[47], a person was targeted by a Chinese headhunter on LinkedIn. It is believed that this person became a target because the individual had nearly a quarter million dollars in debt. What's worse, this person had access to names of American operatives working covertly in China. He was caught and convicted; and now faces the remainder of his life in prison.

The real problem with LinkedIn, from a privacy perspective, is that employees don't just mention where they work. They also

---

[47] NBCUniversal News Group. (2019, April 4). *How a $230,000 debt and a linkedin message led an ex-CIA officer to spy for China*. NBCNews.com. https://www.nbcnews.com/politics/national-security/how-230-000-debt-linkedin-message-led-ex-cia-officer-n990691

talk about what they are working on. Sometimes this is done directly but more often it's done indirectly. Today with the use of AI, it is much easier to summarize a person's LinkedIn profile to gain understanding in what their employer is doing.

The British intelligence service, MI5, estimates that as many as 10,000 professionals in the United Kingdom have have been approached by foreign governments and encouraged to divulge secrets[48]. The MI5 suggests that fake profiles are being produced at an "industrial scale".

One of the problems with social media in general is that the threshold of authentication is low, so it is easily manipulated. This is a specific problem for LinkedIn, where authenticity is almost assumed. People tend to trust LinkedIn profiles.

There was a case where a security company was hired to test an organization's security[49]. One of the things the security experts did did was create a LinkedIn account from a few photos of an attractive woman they found online. Her LinkedIn account was developed into a bio with an impressive education and work history. They aggressively sought connections to this account, including many at the company where they were conducting the penetration test. Once the account had an acceptable number of connections, they changed the account to pose as an employee at the targeted company. They used this account to send holiday wishes (and a harmless piece of malware) throughout the company. Every member of the executive group took the bait, except the Security Manager.

After looking at a few (vainly written) LinkedIn profiles, it's easy to see that often the intended audience is the person

[48]   Corera, G. (2021, April 20). Mi5 warns of spies using linkedin to trick staff into spilling secrets. BBC News. https://www.bbc.com/news/technology-56812746

[49]   Bridges, J. (2021, November 3). *The corporate security risks of being on linkedin*. LinkedIn. https://www.linkedin.com/pulse/corporate-security-risks-being-linkedin-jennifer-bridges/

writing the posts. These are probably the most dangerous from a privacy standpoint because these people aren't aware of who is listening.

Employment advertisements

As an investigator, it's important not to view help wanted ads as places to find employment. Instead, view job postings as lists of skills that the organization currently needs. Additionally, these advertisements identify where they skills are needed.

I always suggest that employment advertisements be done without identifying the company's name. This obviously also means that job postings should not appear on corporate websites. It's far better, from an organizational privacy standpoint, to use websites like: inDeed.com, Monster.com, or Ladders.com.

Maps

Now that maps aren't limited to print, they've become a mashup for presenting any type of geo-related data. The information available on maps has extended to a wide variety of things that weren't found on maps twenty years ago, including:

- User reviews of businesses
- Traffic congestion updates
- Topographic and flood data
- Levels of sound pollution.

Additionally, maps can be combined with other datasources to create maps of things that are not otherwise available, like a map of all ATMs in Afghanistan.

Google Street view

Google's first person map, *Street view,* is very useful when traveling to unfamiliar places. One of my favorite airport lounge activities is to use Street view to plot my path from where I'll be staying to where I need to go.

Google Earth (desktop)

Google Earth is what's known as a *geobrowser,* or software that allows users to explore and visualize geographic information in a three-dimensional globe. There are desktop and browser versions of the product. While both products are impressive, the desktop version allows scrolling forward and backwards through their historic images. In some locations, London for example, this data goes back to the 1940s. This ability allows Journalists to view *map histories* to document the disappearance of villages in areas with border disputes. Business owners may used this to trace the development of competing infrastructure.

Sentinelhub

The advantage to *Sentinelhub*, over *Google Earth*, is that it has better date resolution. While Google Earth allows historic views, it's resolution is counted in months and years. Sentinelhub, in contrast, updates information as often as daily.

One of the more interesting features of Sentinelhub is that it provides access to the satellite's infrared cameras. These infrared views are primarily used to detect agriculture. This could perhaps be a valuable source of intelligence for commodities traders or anyone involved in agriculture.

Sentinelhub also facilitates a "fire filter" that makes it easy to spot fires. This feature, along with the ability to look back in time, has led to some interesting studies of how forest fires spread.

IP addresses and geo data

A long time ago, I sold a service that plotted the location of web visitors on a map. This was accomplished by obtaining the domain name associated with the web surfer's IP address through a process known as a *reverse IP lookup*. Once I knew the domain associated with the IP address, I could use that information to discover ownership of the domain and the zip code of origin.

Geo coordinates for every US Zip code.

A weighted dot on the map was relative to the number of hits at that zip code. While this was an useful service, the rapid increase in private domain registration and VPNs put an end to a cool little application.

XIF data

Earlier we talked about XIF, and how it was a format for containing metadata of digital photographs. One of the more popular XIF properties are the geo coordinates of where a photo was taken. From an intelligence perspective, XIF codes can either verify where an image was created, or put that claim into question.

One of the more famous examples of using XIFs as intelligence was before the current phase of the Ukraine/Russian war. At

179

that time, Russia denied that they had troops on Ukrainian soil. This claim was put into question when Russian troops posted XIF-coded selfies on social media[50] that clearly revealing their position in Ukraine.

Affiliate data

Affiliate programs are designed to pay affiliates to drive traffic to their website. I have seen affiliate programs unintentionally provide remarkable industry intelligence though these services. If there is an affiliate service remotely connected to your industry, it may be worth investigation.

Crowdsourcing

It is often thought that crowd of random people will collectively have more intellectual power than individual experts[51]. This *wisdom of the crowds* is now conveniently displayed on: Indiegogo.com or GoFundMe.com.

Crowdfunding originally was a way to test new ideas without a lot of money. Marketers, however, quickly learned that this is also a great way to launch an already funded (new) product. As such, crowdfunding sites are a good place to gauge public acceptance of new product ideas.

Specialized sources

The Internet is loaded with specialized websites designed to retrieve very specific data. If your objectives align with one of these sources, you're in luck. A few are identified below. These resources come and go. But the community also maintains a current list on GitHub.

---

[50] Schogol, J. (2023, January 3). *Russian soldier gave away his position with geotagged social media posts*. Task & Purpose. https://taskandpurpose.com/news/russian-military-opsec-failure-ukraine/

[51] Surowiecki, J. (2005). *The Wisdom of Crowds*. Anchor Books.

Finding documents

In *Section II: Tactics*, you learn how to search for specific file types. You should also know that there are complete libraries of digital documents, online. One of the larger ones is scridb.com, a searchable library of over 170 million documents. If your interests are other people's slide presentations, there also a collection of presentations at slideshare.net.

The website searchcode.com, claims to be able to find unprotected (public) documents on Google Drive. These would include: spreadsheets, presentations, and text documents.

Published leaks

While you've all heard about Wikileaks.org, there are also lesser known websites that publish leaked information. For example, offShoreLeaks.icij.org, is maintained by they International Consortium of Investigative Journalists.

Sometimes leaks inform the public of things they need to be informed of. Other times, they are leaks of connivence and only make public safety that much harder to maintain, as was the case with the spate of leaked NSA tools[52]. I'll leave the ethics of using leaked intelligence up to you.

Pastebins and Chans

Pastebins are online services where users can store and share plain text. It's particularly useful for quickly sharing things like source code snippets during discussions on platforms like Internet Relay Chat (IRC). Pastebins tend to live on the edge of the Internet, and are often used by hacking groups, particularly to publicize or take credit for exploits.

It's probably best to think of *"Chan pages"*, like 4chan.org as

---

[52] exploits, T. (n.d.). *NSA's powerful Windows Hacking Tools leaked online.* CNNMoney. https://money.cnn.com/2017/04/14/technology/windows-exploits-shadow-brokers/index.html

the pastebins of social media. I think that's a fair description.

Code searches

There are search engines that specifically look for source code. These could be useful if your developer needs code to perform a classic function. The website searchcode.com, for example, boasts the ability to, "search 75 billion lines of code from 40 million projects." Another online tool, grep.app, allows users to search through the vast *git repositories*.

The network as a data source

Not only does the Internet facilitate much of today's competitive intelligence, but we can also use infrastructure itself as an intelligence source.

A major piece of infrastructure that can be investigated is *DNS* or the *Domain Name System.* DNS is like the phone book of the Internet, and converts easy-to-remember domain names into difficult to remember and constantly changing network addresses. But you can also use DNS in unprescribed ways to tell if two organizations are in communication.

The exploit works like this, but it only works with organizations that host their own Domain Name Server. Since it takes time to convert a domain name into network addresses, DNS servers will store a local copy of the network address in cache for the next time it needs it. The result is that it takes much less time to pull an address out of cache than it takes to get the same information form the Domain Name System. If the amount of time to convert the domain are the same on the first and second conversion, you can assume that the conversion was pulled from cache and not the DNS system. That means that these two organizations communicated before you conducted the exploit.

Another example of using the network as a data source is to ping a server periodically to see how long it takes to respond.

Recorded delays can indicate the times of day that the server is most busy.

Finding the owners of domains

Domain names are clues to organizations aspirations. Marketing departments will reserve domain names well in advance of registering trademarks. Because, if you can't secure the domain name for a website, you don't need the trademark. As such, organizations announce their plans in the Domain Name System long before they make the product commercially available. This gives competition organizations time to react.

If you're interested in knowing what domain names your competitor owns, the tool analyzeid.com may be for you.

There was a time that it was easy to find aspirational moves through domain name registrations. For example, I did a workshop for Investigative Journalists in London where I asked journalists to document when Sarah Palin, a 2008 US vice-presidential candidate first showed signs of presidential aspirations. This task was selected because she claimed she had no such presidential plans. From the DNS records, we were able to find domain names (like PalinForPresident.com) secured by her campaign manager, in 2006 just after she was elected Governor of Alaska.

Odds and ends

Intelligence exists where you don't expect it. While we see rendered webpages in browsers, there is sometimes information in the webpage that is never seen. Sometimes information takes the form of poorly written JavaScript that reveals private APIs or insights into how data is structure internally in databases. Other times, like the example below, there is information in the programming comments.

```
              88
              88
              88
 ,adPPYba,  88,dPPYba,   ,adPPYYba,  8b        d8
a8P_____88  88P'   "8a  ""     `Y8  `8b      d8'
8PP"""""""  88       d8  ,adPPPPP88   `8b    d8'
"8b,   ,aa  88b,   ,a8"  88,    ,88    `8b,d8'
 `"Ybbd8"'  8Y"Ybbd8"'   `"8bbdP"Y8      Y88'
                                          d8'
                                         d8'

Now hiring @ http://jobs.ebaycareers.com/

Want to help build the home page? http://www.ebaynyc.com/jobs
```

A job posting made public in HTML source code

Further thoughts

Sometimes it's unavoidable to have one sole data sources for a campaign, but it's never ideal. You should always strive to obtain multiple or backup sources for intelligence gathering.

Having a back-up source of information can be a campaign saver once a prime source goes away, or when the source changes and a tactic no longer works.

The other advantage to having multiple intelligence sources is that the more useful data you collect, the more statistically accurate it becomes.

Chapter 10: Finding sources

C hapter 11
Handling intellectual property

Investigators became dependent on resources found on the Internet when competitive intelligence transitioned from the physical to virtual worlds. This change increased both the quantity and quality of intelligence available to investigators.

But anonymous and automated tactics also changed the way investigators interact with their sources. These new methods made it easier to violate other people's intellectual property rights.

In *Chapter 8, Tactics and ethics*, you read about guidelines for using online services. This chapter describes what you can and can't do with the data found on websites. This *intellectual property* includes: *patents, copyrights, trademarks, and trade secrets*. These guidelines apply for both virtual and physical investigations.

> *Please don't confuse this chapter for legal advice. Seek council before you need it.*

Like Chapter 8, this chapter is a set of armchair opinions from a guy that has received some advice and has had a few experiences. For whatever my journey is worth, it certainly won't help you pass the Bar Exam. It's better to think of this chapter as helpful tips and not legal guidance.

There are legal risks in conducting competitive intelligence and in running bots, if you choose to do so. As an investigator, you need to strike a balance. You shouldn't exaggerate or downplay the legal exposure that comes with bot development. Personally, I've been fortunate, I haven't encountered any serious legal problems. But that's partly because I've been cautious and sought advice from experts outside my area of expertise.

Perhaps the closest thing to legal advice you'll read here is that attorneys tend to be very cautious about legal matters. If they believe you've violated their clients' rights, they won't hesitate to take legal action. So, it's a good idea to learn about the relevant laws and know what questions to ask when seeking legal help.

IP rights

The easiest way to think about *Intellectual Property*, or *IP*, is that it is a catch-all phrase for a group of assets where the owner has obtained legal monopolies for their use or distribution. For example, a pharmaceutical company may have exclusive rights to manufacture and market a new drug. In another case, IP rights may give an author exclusive authority to use a script. With the exception of Trademarks and Trade Secrets, these monopolies expire at some point.

From the stand point of competitive intelligence, the two forms of IP that are the most pertinent are copyrights and trade secrets.

Copyright

Under copyright law, the creator of an original work is granted exclusive rights to reproduce, distribute, publicly display or perform, and create derivative works based on the original work. These rights allow the creator to control how their work is used, shared, and monetized, and to protect their work from unauthorized copying or use.

Copyright protection lasts for a limited period, usually the life of the author plus a certain number of years after their death (typically 70 years in the United States and many other countries)[53]. After the copyright term expires, the work enters the public domain, and anyone can freely use, share, or build upon the work without needing permission from the original creator.

Exceptions to copyright

Copyright law has exceptions that allow the use of copyrighted material without the need for explicit permission from the copyright holder. Some of the key exceptions are outlined below.

You cannot copyright a fact

It is important to note that copyright law protects the expression of ideas, not the ideas themselves[54]. That means you cannot copyright a fact. Since much of what competitive intelligence campaigns collects are facts, you shouldn't be prevented by any law from using most of the intelligence you collect.

Facts are considered objective pieces of information, independent of any individual's creative expression. And for that reason are considered part of the public domain. As such, anyone is free to use, share, or build upon them. Granting copyright protection to facts would be a bad idea as it would hinder the free flow of information and restrict access to knowledge.

---

[53] *How long does a copyright last.* Copyright Alliance. (2023, June 15). https://copyrightalliance.org/faqs/how-long-does-copyright-last

[54] *What does copyright protect?.* What Does Copyright Protect? (FAQ) | U.S. Copyright Office. (n.d.). https://www.copyright.gov/help/faq/faq-protect.html

A partial list of facts that are commonly collected during a competitive intelligence campaign include:

- Prices
- Product names
- Inventory availability
- Logistics paths.

While facts themselves have no intellectual property protection, the way they are presented does. The explanation for how presentation and content obtain different levels of protection is to say that:

> The words in a dictionary aren't protected, but their definitions are.
>
> The content of a mailing list isn't protectable, but it's organization may be.
>
> The paintings in a coffee table book of the US Revolutionary War are by now all in the public domain, but the way they are formatted in the book is protected by copyright.

Fair use

Fair use allows for the use of copyrighted material for purposes such as criticism, commentary, news reporting, teaching, scholarship, and research. Here are some of the factors that determine fair use.

> Much of the determination into what's fair use involves intent. If it's for something like education or news it's usually permissible.
>
> The nature of the use is also protected. Courts tend not to stop comedic or satiric uses of material.
>
> Another factor that affects fair use is the amount of content borrowed. A small clip of a book review is generally acceptable but reprinting an entire chapter, probably not.

When courts consider damages to copyright, they usually take into consideration the affect that an infringement had on the original owner's market for the material. This may leave the impression that if damages are small, or can't be determined, that there's no case. But large organizations, like Disney, aggressively prosecute copyright infringement, even from small players.

Public Domain

Works in the *public domain* are not protected by copyright and are free for anyone to use. Works in the public domain include expired copyrights and collections that were never eligible for copyright protection, and instances where copyright holder has relinquished their rights. The duration of copyright protection varies depending on the medium, so you may be able to use intellectual property that received copyright protection many years ago, but it's always advisable to verify the status beforehand.

Knowing what intellectual property is going into public domain status could be a competitive advantage for an organization, depending on the industry.

Government publications are some of the most useful areas of the public domain. In the USA, census results are particularly useful.

News reporting

Using copyrighted material in journalism is generally allowed, as long as it is used to inform the public about current events. This would include the use of short quotes in book reviews, or show movie clips in theater commentary.

Time shifting

Time shifting refers to making personal copies of copyrighted material for later viewing or listening. For example, it's usually acceptable to record a TV show to time shift and watch later, or ripping a CD to listen to in your car. The implication, however, is that the person doing the time shifting has legal use of the media and that time shifting is the only use of the copied media.

Trade secrets

Trades secrets are those techniques and processes that give one business a competitive advantage over another. Trade secrets are well named because they loose their value once discovered by their competitors. That's why trade secrets are never published like other intellectual property.

Examples of trade secrets include:

- Chanel's perfume formulas
- Google's search algorithms
- A journalist's list of sources

Trade secrets are protected through confidentiality and security measures. It's important to organizations to take active steps to keep their trade secrets secret. Some of the steps an organization can take to help ensure the agency of their trade secrets include:

- Implementing robust internal policies for the non-disclosure of sensitive information
- Properly labeling trade secrets
- Restricting access to sensitive information

Reverse engineered trade secrets

While obtaining trade secrets through theft is illegal, it is perfectly acceptable to appropriate trade secrets through experimentation and *reverse engineering*. Reverse engineering involves independently analyzing a product or process to understand how it works.

Trade secrets can be reverse engineered without access to the original design documents or proprietary information. In the context of trade secrets, reverse engineering can be both a legitimate practice and a potential risk to those that hold trade secrets.

Independent discovery of trade secrets

Trade secrets are protected under trade secret law as long as they remain secret and the owner takes reasonable steps to keep them confidential. However, trade secret protection does not prevent others from independently developing or discovering the same information through lawful means.

If you independently and legitimately discover a trade secret without any prior knowledge of it, you are not bound by any obligation of confidentiality or restrictions. You are free to use and exploit that information for your own purposes, even if it is the same as someone else's trade secret.

Trade secrets and competitive intelligence

As you may have guessed, trade secrets are at the very center of competitive intelligence. If you're fortunate, you'll be able to uncover trade secrets and use them to your advantage.

Misappropriation

Declaring something a trade secret gives an organization the right to protect it from theft. Trade secret theft, also known as misappropriation, occurs when someone gains unauthorized access to confidential information. This would include situations were physical files are stolen or networks are hacked.

A famous case of a misappropriated trade secret involved Coca-Cola and PepsiCo[55]. In that case, a disgruntled Coca-Cola

---

[55]   NBC Universal News Group. (2007, February 1). *Ex-secretary guilty in theft of Coca-Cola Secrets.* NBCNews.com. https://www.nbcnews.com/id/wbna16930151

employee decided to take revenge on her employer. She had access to trade secrets, and thought that she could sell them to the competitor, Pepsi. In doing so, she could both retaliate against her employer while putting away a potential financial windfall at the same time.

While she had a lot of enthusiasm for her objective, she lacked a tactic. But she did know a guy that just got out of prison, who led her to a guy who could help.

Once onboard, the ex-con wrote an unusually random letter to Pepsi, saying he had Coca-Cola trade secrets for sale. When the letter made it's way to a PepsiCo executive, his first phone call was to Coca-Cola, and their second call was to the FBI.

An FBI agent, now appearing as a Pepsi executive, arranged to meet the ex-convict at the Atlanta airport. Once they met, the special agent was handed a bag, supposedly filled with Coca-Cola trade secrets. In the exchange, the undercover agent provided a Girl Scout Cookie box stuffed with $75,000 in currency.

While reports don't mention specifics, we know that both the former Coca-Cola employee and her convict friend both went to prison, and that she was sentenced to eight years of confinement.

Case studies: more misappropriation

As mentioned at the start of this book, the only competitive intelligence campaigns that the public hears about are when organizations that get caught breaking the law. While this imbalanced reporting causes a public relations problem for competitive intelligence, it also provides lessons.

The following are some reported cases, regarding the illegal capture of information, that have been publicly reported.

In 2019, Dominion Energy Inc. accepted bids for a gas turbine plant. After the bids were cast, one Dominion employee and one Siemens employee were convicted of a conspiracy to steal trade secrets from General Electric and Mitsubishi[56]. In this case, the Siemens employee became friendly with the Dominion representative that was receiving the bids. So much so, that they were talked into sharing details of the GE and Mitsubishi bids with the Siemens employee. In exchange, the Dominion representative received gifts, including: tickets to sporting events, hotel rooms, and dinners.

In a court deposition, the Siemens employee stated that he had received bid information from Dominion and discreetly distributed it to their staff. As a result, they lowered their bid below those of GE and Mitsubishi, and won the contract. When asked if he would have lowered the bid if they hadn't had access to the bidding data, he said, "Probably not." Siemens wasn't held liable, but the Siemens employee involved with the caper was. This was largely due to the fact that Siemens actually found the infraction during an internal audit, and reported it.

In another case, DuPont accused Kolon Industries of stealing trade secrets related to the production of Kevlar[57], a high-strength synthetic fiber used in a variety of products ranging from body armor to automotive seatbelts. Kolon Industries was developing an alternative to Kevlar named Heracron. According to the statement filed with the court, Kolon conspired with former DuPont employees to steal DuPont's trade secrets for making Kevlar. The company was sentenced to pay $85 million in criminal fines and $275 million in restitution.

---

[56]   Jahner, K., & Hughes, S. (2023, October 26). *Siemens Exec charged in conspiracy to steal GE Trade Secrets (1)*. Bloomberg Law. https:// news.bloomberglaw.com/ip-law/energy-executive-charged-in-conspiracy-to-steal-ge-trade-secrets

[57]   https://www.justice.gov/opa/pr/kolon-industries-inc-pleads-guilty-conspiring-steal-dupont-trade-secrets-involving-kevlar

You can leave an employer, but you can't take their trade secrets with you. In 2014, Toshiba alleged that a former SanDisk engineer had secretly taken confidential information about their flash memory technology and given it to SK Hynix. They claimed that SK Hynix had used this information to develop its own flash memory chips, which it then sold at lower prices than Toshiba. The lawsuits were eventually settled out of court. It is believed that SK Hynix paid a significant amount of money to Toshiba to resolve the dispute.

Copyrights & trade secrets compared

As a recap, it might be useful to see how copyright and trade secrets compare in a side-by-side comparison, as performed below.

	Copyrights	Trade secrets
Scope	Legal monopolies for creative works	Protections for organizational secrets like formulas and processes
Infringement	Unauthorized use	Obtained through theft, misappropriation, or violation of NDA
Duration	Expire	Never expire
Disclosure	Public	Private
Registration	Automatic	None required
Appropriation	Can be used under fair use laws.	Can be appropriated through discovery and reverse engineering.
Enforcement	Enforced through copyright laws	Mainly enforced through confidentiality

Comparisons of copyright and trade secret law

Further thoughts

Intellectual property rights aren't that hard to figure out. Unless you plan to resell someone else's IP, or pretend that it's your own, you're not apt to violate anyone's ownership rights.

Perhaps the most important thing to draw from this chapter is that all facts are in the public domain. But, if you discover a fact before everyone else, that becomes a trade secret, and you are not obligated to share it with anyone.

The other important point is that trade secrets are normally protected through: policy, *confidentiality agreements*, non-disclosure agreements, and employment contracts.

I hope this book is an important branch on your journey through competitive intelligence. Now that we've met, don't be a stranger. Please feel free to contact me at mike@mepso.com if you find errata, have questions, or just want to chat.

—mgs,

IN CLOSING

Competitive intelligence is a crucial field that involves gathering data and insights about your competitors. The analysis of intelligence is the very lifeblood of competition. When done well, competitive intelligence provides a path for continual organizational improvement that should make things better for all of us.

Is competition good?

The endorsement of competitive intelligence has been based on the premise that competitive intelligence drives competition and that competition is good. But is it?

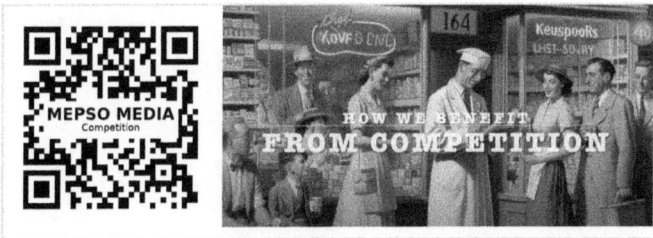

Use QR code to access video, "From Physical to Virtual"

Listed below are a few ways that we benefit from healthy competition.

When there's competition, people try to outperform each other. This drive leads to continuous innovation, improvement, and better products all around.

When there are multiple competitive suppliers in the same market, prices tend to decrease. So not only does competition lead to products that more closely meet consumer needs, those products also become more affordable.

Competition forces organizations to streamline their processes and reduce waste. Efficiency gains lead to cost savings, which can benefit customers, employees, and management.

Organizations also hire and retain talent to gain a competitive edge. As a result, competitive markets create demand for skilled workers. Job opportunities increase, benefiting individuals and the overall economy.

About the author

Spying on Success is Michael Schrenk's sixth book on data collection and analysis. Unlike his prior books that explain the technical aspects of bot development, *Spying on Success* compiles nearly thirty years of experience of developing and conducting competitive intelligence campaigns.

	**Spying on Success** *Competitive Intelligence in the age of Artificial Intelligence* First & Second Editions 2024 & 2025 Mepso Media
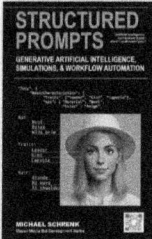	**Structured Prompts** *Generative Artificial Intelligence, Simulations, and Workflow Automation* 2025, Mepso Media
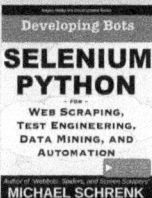	**Developing Bots with Selenium Python** *For Web Scraping, Test Engineering, Data Mining, and Automation* 2023, Mepso Media
	**Webbots, Spiders and Screen Scrapers** *A guide to developing Internet Agents in PHP-Curl* First & Second Editions Multiple languages 2007 & 2012, No Starch Press

Mike is a sought after consultant and keynote speaker and has influenced decision makers everywhere from Moscow to Silicon Valley. He is particularly proud to be a nine-time DEF CON speaker.

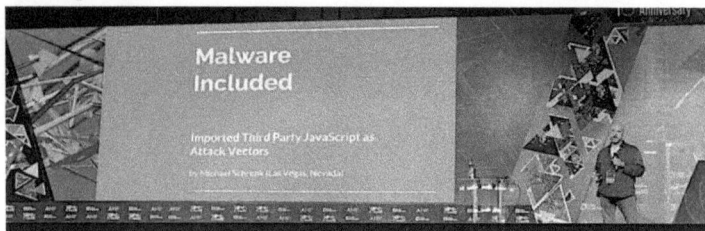

Java2Days/CodeMonsters, The National Palace of Culture, Sofia Bulgaria

Mike lives in the Southwest USA with his lovely wife and fearless chihuahua. When he's not developing competitive intelligence campaigns, you can find him playing guitar or driving (repairing) his vintage British sports car.

Please contact the author at: mike@mepso.com.

Related resources

Spying on Success also includes a growing collection of related videos. These related resources are available at the publisher's website.

Spying on Success

Index